YOKE

&

FEATHER

ESSAYS

JESSIE VAN EERDEN

DZANC
BOOKS

DZANC
BOOKS

2580 Craig Rd.
Ann Arbor, MI 48103
www.dzancbooks.org

Library of Congress Cataloging-in-Publication Data Available on Request

ISBN 9780984213368
First edition: November 2024
Cover design by Steven Seighman
Interior design by Michelle Dotter

Cover image Copyright © Mary E. Zompetti: "Rose of Sharon, Heatwave
and No Rain; July 16–August 11, 2021, Roanoke, VA"

Printed in the United States of America

10   9   8   7   6   5   4   3   2   1

for my brothers—Jake, Luke, and Daniel

CONTENTS

*Gravity makes things come down, wings make them rise:
What wings raised to the second power can make things
come down without weight? ...Grace is the law of the
descending movement.*

—Simone Weil, *Gravity and Grace*

PROLOGUE

*And there was a woman who had had a discharge of blood for
twelve years... She had heard the reports about Jesus and came
up behind him in the crowd and touched his garment... And immediately the flow of blood dried up, and she felt in her body that
she was healed of her disease. And Jesus, perceiving in himself that
power had gone out from him, immediately turned about in the
crowd and said, "Who touched my garments?"*

—Gospel of Mark 5:25-30, English Standard Version

PUT YOUR HANDS AT THE HIP YOKE, she says, above the lapped V-
seam where the skirt gathers then flares. You feel where the womb
waits? Where the weight gets carried? This is the center of all gravity. You feel it? She guides his palm with both her hands to the
yoke of her dress. The young man blushes and tucks his face away.
Her feet are flat on the road, straddling her bicycle, dress bunched
up. She releases the warm hand of the stranger walking by and
returns her hands to the handlebars.

You feel it, she says, as he hurries off like a lamb.

Every so often along this road by the sea she does this, stops
the forward movement of time—time that unmakes our skin and
sight and takes in our finite heartbeats like someone filling a basket
of barley—and she touches a stranger. Sometimes she puts both
hands on his face as if a lover, sometimes she traces a woman's

lifeline, sometimes she meets a young man like this one, with a shy face under a derby cap, who blushes when suddenly they are no longer strangers.

She pedals on. The jasmine blossoms quiver in the bicycle basket, peeking from the paper.

Can I come? her son asked.

Not this time, maybe next. She kissed his hot eyes, he toddled into her legs to hug goodbye with face and body, all his small strong bones.

She pedals on, comes to the wide place at the mountain's base. There is no throng, but she pictures the throng. She leans her bicycle against a cedar and departs from its shade into the sun with her cut jasmine. It happened here, and she closes her eyes to hear the voices and scuffling soles, the forceful presence of bodies, and to feel herself again an emaciated husk of woman, eyes hollow, skin like crusts of bread, when she moved through the crowd without memory or plan. They raised their many voices to someone coming. She saw him in profile, hair simple and dark, shoulders narrow, he was not large. Despite the crowd, he seemed to be among no one, like a man on the shore watching the boats raise their sails. She felt nothing, her fingers curled like prawns. She was carried by the crowd's current, and he passed by with his simple body walking.

She kneels in the dust and presses her face to the huddle of tiny blossoms wrapped in paper, white with a blush of yellow at each center.

When he walked by, she felt as though she had passed through a curtain of ribbons, each stitched with a line of lilies wilting, like a beaded curtain leading into a back room but unstrung with beads and sewn with flower petals. Their softness touched everywhere her face, so many petals grazing her face like little hands. The cur-

tain of his sadness—she passed through, and on the other side of
the curtain, the air in the back room was all changed air, charged
with her own sadness, her twelve years of hair and flesh going to
dull metal, and before that, the years of all she ever was—girl on
bike, girl tasting fig, girl spitting venom, girl with hem high slip
shown slipped up, woman coming, O the tip of her life—then the
menses draining, twelve years *niddah*, untouched, with blood that
would not stop.

She stanched it with rags, raw cotton, with sheep's wool. Untouched, she stemmed the flow alone, knitted pads of rabbit fur,
scrub grass, moss. She ran from the city when she still had strength
to run, out onto the dunes where she let the blood drain out and
blacken the sand like animal dung, and she reached down to dip,
touched it to her wasting cheeks like rouge, like war paint, like
she was mask-making. *Niddah, niddah*, her life iron, her deepest
food a filth, drained but never dry. For her inner thighs there was
no bath, no *mikveh*, immersion and rising up pure and touchable,
only plunge baths in the cattle trough and the swamp eddies, soaking until she stained the water red.

Because she felt all that when he passed by with his sadness-
curtain of a hundred petals on her face, with his eternity in a vis-
cous skin sack holding all of time so she remembered so he remembered so he could hold her sadness—*because he can hold my
sadness*—her hand went out for a clutch of his coat—wait. Wait.

The hem was rough in her hand. It happened in a moment,
the backward rush of twelve years, the feel of the inward blooming
bath, a wash, up through capillary marrow lobe and dark lip: some
girl on bike, some woman tipping falling into green grass, womb
like plum and other fruit again, like unwithered night.

Who touched me? he asked in the horde that flanked and
hounded him on all sides, because he knew what touch is. Her lips
red with shock. His blush to show the fury of the flood.

No one knew her name. When the wind blew west she was Martha, when it blew east she was Beronike and later Veronica, *Vera Icon*, true image, true face. In encyclopedias and church records in basements, in whispers of relics and cloths with secret properties, she spanned legends. She was said to be pious, to be there with her white veil to wipe the blood from his forehead when he'd had too much sadness to hold, and the veil she pulled back bore the imprint of his face. In the Greek, in the Latin, in the third-century pages of the bishop Eusebius who went himself to the old Roman city, to the base of Mount Hermon, and said he saw she had made two statues of half-finished faces at the gate of her house: a woman bent, a man about to touch. The bishop wiped the snow from the bronze faces himself, the patina arresting, his own memory suddenly aching.

But no one really knew her name. She had lovers after, she had a child, a son. She put her hand on her boy's head, where he sat with the other children—You feel that? she asked. She fluttered her hand on the top of his coarse-cropped hair to say, I choose you—Duck, Duck, Duck, Goose, I anoint you, the center of all, the great risk of joy. She loved to touch strangers, on the face, the back, the wrist.

She leaves her paper of jasmine in the dust and pedals home. She will come again soon with a clutch of lily and rose mallow, snapdragon and phlox, a mayapple with one pop of white—one day maybe with her child. Hyacinths, hibiscus, tulips and the damask rose, carnations, cabbage flowers sometimes, and sometimes orchid. All the upturned skirts, the cups of want creased at the stem like skirts at the yoke of the dress—all the blossoms in the basket of her bike for him because he remembers, he whose sadness passes by. Because he knows what flowers are, that they are tiny hands touching.

I.

A BLESSING BOOK

MEET ME AT THE DOLLAR GENERAL
ACROSS FROM THE FAMILY DOLLAR

when Jesus comes back, and we'll see what really happens to one another's bodies. I mean, will we get some relief? Will we fade to ether, or will it be more like: the body as dog wants in so badly and, finally, you don't just *let* it in, you *carry* it in, all mange and burr and fat deer tick, all thousand ditches slept in, and you think, *That there is my body*, and you say, *You're home now, buddy.* I guess I mean, will we forgive our flesh its loneliness and burn? Or maybe in the New Heaven and the New Earth we'll simply reverse time— it's back to girlhood's Smurfette shirt and white-blonde hair and hands wrapping the meat of a brother's kill and hands in the creek with the leeches and the crawdads and a plastic ring from either dollar store in our West Virginia town with its charismatic church camp that folds dreams of Apocalypse into our heads, snug as raisins in monkey bread, and we'll start all over.

BUT RIGHT NOW, SINCE THERE'S a haggardness to our bodies and since Jesus is taking his time, meet me at the Dollar General to go on a mission to buy tubes of Soft Lips with our allowance, then we'll cross to the Family Dollar for Wet 'n' Wild burgundy lipstick that makes us look like death. We can twist it up all the way then cap it hard to watch the smoosh-volcano of glistening burgundy through the transparent top. Which is to ask you: right now, through your burgundy lips, what's the prayer you've got going? For it's *this* earth and it's *this* pain and it's *this* body breaking open to be reckoned with. I mean, more precisely, can you help me pray now for the now, and say to the monstrous body, *You are not monstrous*, and help me to know love in the midst of going long untouched and in the midst of terror that the body might not be touched again after the divorce or after somebody lying near, under the sky in the sky, leaves, and in the midst of all our respective terrors of never having a child or losing custody or getting sick? For today is the divorce and the court date and the empty womb and the biopsy. What I mean is a kind of prayer as healing even as you die your death, prayer as becoming whole even as you tatter and tatter. The kind of prayer that is a brittle bread, but at least it's real bread.

As FAR AS PRAYERS GO, I'm talking about a letting-loose-within-the-dwelling-deep kind. A leap not into disappearance but into wrangling a good roundoff back handspring and feeling both the flight and the landing and practicing it daily, like the girl on the corner of Pocahontas and Preston with her pooched little-girl belly and her ecstatic face that says *The first sky I saw was the sky inside me*. I love how she takes up space in the middle of the street where the ambulance goes and my neighbor Mack's electric wheelchair goes and the Harley two doors down and Cathy who totters off on foot to the dollar store before the weather changes in the way her joints predict. The girl is out there even when the weather has changed for the worse—no matter; it's do or die, in that moment of leap, and the girl doesn't even have a spotter at her tumbling mat spread on the dirty pavement. She raises Mary Lou Retton arms, gets a running start, corkscrews down to land on palm and fingertips, then bounces down-up on her rubber toes and goes back for the handspring, light as a sack of feathers, and ends panting and beaming. She pulls her shirt down and takes it again from the top.

I WANT TO PRAY LIKE THIS IMPORTUNATE TUMBLER-BODY, with her letting-go that gives herself as a gift to herself, because, recently, a man lay with me under the sky in the sky then left an emptiness. He and I woke early to ride bicycles to the James Turrell Skyspace installation; it was after dawn but early enough to have the dome to ourselves so we could lie side by side, but apart, under the oval aperture in the ceiling. The concrete cold, our caps as rough pillows. To have the sky framed alters the sky, makes it seem fuller and more potent, and so made me feel fuller and more potent, all things promising. I thought: This body by mine, who might we become to each other? I had thought about it over tacos, during sex, during the challenge of cake baking when he had no sugar or a mixer in the house but only avocadoes and mountains of books. Thought it hopefully in bed while the projector from the library broadcasted the French film large as life on the white sheet tacked to his wall.

A BIRD DARTED ACROSS THE SKYSPACE OPENING, then a jet's contrail: first, like an incision, and then, before our eyes, it diffused into feather. Soon, it was over. Soon, he was gone. I went to Spain, and I carried a yearning for him to Spain though I prayed not to, but that is a different kind of prayer than the one I'm discussing here. After dinner one night, my Parisian friend showed a few of us his experimental film on his laptop. He had made masks of faces and put them underwater, and what did they naturally do? The lips tried to kiss lips, cheek tried to touch cheek, in the buoyancy of water. There were no unnatural smiles, the eyes were closed, the soft lips could not part, but it was one of the tenderest things in the world, I thought, as the MacBook glowed and my friend talked about working for five years making photographic portraits of people with disfigured faces to say they are not monstrous. I saw the photos; theirs were bodies more disrupted than most, cell division compromised beyond repair, but all our bodies, with teeth loosening and joints inflaming, are headed to monstrosity, to a place beyond repair. I touched my face and thought about the French film projected onto the wall and the minor folds in the sheet wrinkling the actresses' skin as though it were real skin like his and mine, not so young anymore, or so lovely. Of course they are not monstrous, but do we believe it? Do they? They are not monstrous. They are not monstrous. Saying it again and again is a prayer that is like the masks hovering in water for so many consecutive minutes, kissing but not kissing.

TODAY I MEANT TO WRITE AN ESSAY ON PRAYER, not fool around with this business of the Apocalypse and the dollar stores and a breakup. But, anyway, this is the essay I've begun.

AS FAR AS PRAYERS GO, I want to pray you into a clean little room and say: Here is a dresser for you with little knobs on the drawers, a small mirror on a stand, a place to live your life, a place for making and displaying homemade cards. Here is a sink to use and daily dinner together with the napkin folded in a rose around a ripe cherry still on its stem.

OR, RATHER, I PRAY YOUR SUFFERING BODY—your good body which is a monstrous body which is not at all a monstrous body—be a dwelling place for God, if you're willing. In *An Interrupted Life*, the diary of the Dutch Jewish woman Etty Hillesum, regarding the decimated jasmine behind her house, Etty wrote, *Somewhere inside me the jasmine continues to blossom undisturbed.* Etty wrote to God, *We must help you and defend your dwelling place inside us to the last…I shall try to make you at home always.* She meant to make God at home in the body which is the very seat of insatiable yearning and irrevocable dying; it is the body headed for the gas. And when she was finally pressed onto the train from Camp Westerbork to Auschwitz on September 7, 1943, she threw a postcard from the train window that said: *Christine,...I am sitting on my rucksack in the middle of a full freight car. Father, Mother, and Mischa are a few cars away... We left the camp singing.* Farmers found it and posted it on September 15 and Etty died on November 30, but even dying she made God at home, with dressers with their little knobs inside her body, singing on her way to a death camp. Singing does not stop you from dying, prayer does not stop you from hurting, but maybe it breaks you open so you are large enough to bear God inside where the jasmine still stubbornly blooms *just as profusely and delicately as ever it did.* The bread is brittle, but at least it's real bread.

I THINK ABOUT THE FIFTH SUNDAY SING, when our churches on rural mountain charges that are never full of bodies come across a month with a lucky fifth Sunday, and that Sunday night the whole charge comes together to pack the house. The good of the good clothes fills the room. I wear my best bra with no safety pin and hold the shape-note tunebook of old sanguine Charles Wesley hymns, my earlobes pulsing greenish from dollar-store earrings, my lips burgundy. There is no sermon, no instruction, only song after song, the time signatures all determined less by the book than by the rhythm of snapping towels to hang on the wash line, kneading dough to rise in the stout bowl, and it's a plodding sound but also like a heartbeat. All the bodies in polyester dresses or short-sleeved button-up shirts with ties. Fathers with those fatherly watches that say I have to do taxes and I fear death and there is a stranglehold in clerking the store nine to five for so many dull years, but I sweetly and huskily come and come into your mother in the dark to make you and your sister and your brothers, and I can push you so far in the swing that I run underneath you and let you go high into the air so that, as you fall back, harnessed in the swing, the wind wraps your white-blonde hair around your face as a gauzy curtain through which you see the sun and my back and arms still raised from raising you up, as if in praise or surrender. Piano untuned, song after song, so many open throats like those of baby birds not yet with their feather coats.

But what we all wait for at the Sing is Franklin Dixon's solo. He is an oak barrel of wine singing through his nose in a way I love unendingly, the forceful "When We All Get to Heaven" about the place prepared for us, where Jesus will take us when he comes back. We wait for this moment of the night because even though the lyrics with their sentimental rhymes speak to a future, the song itself, its sound and crescendo, prepares a place here for God in the present, on the warm bed of our breath, the *herm* and *herm* building to a twang of word, Franklin hefting up into a note like a large body into the cab of a pickup and us inevitably joining in. Paperback hymnals come apart, but nobody needs the hymnal anyway. We are all saying, Come and dwell here, God, in our now, for we are giving ourselves as gifts to ourselves, our bodies in this polyester and cotton and older flesh once younger—we can bear you in our dying, you infinite intolerable thing.

And so just when I think maybe it's true that I'll never be touched again, not the way he touched me, writing to me once *I will take a feather to your body*—just when I think I'm out of chances and I'm ready to feel sorry for myself, I open the screen door and walk out to the morning world and somehow I am handled all over. I am touched a thousand ways by the waking prayers of the girl doing her roundoff and by a stranger who waves and it's like I can bed down in the crippling warmth of his wave. And there's an intimate stroke of jockey shorts pinned to the neighbor's wash line and a boy who says he'll race me to the pond in his good clothes. Cathy calls out to predict a cold front rolling in. Mack's electric wheelchair runs out of juice on the street outside my house. He usually plugs in at Hardee's but people were in his spot. He tells

me, as I try to push him home, that he was a deejay when Michael
Jackson's records were first coming out, and he loves to dance. He
futilely operates his chair controls with one hand and holds, in
the other, two boxes of Twinkies from the dollar store which is on
the way back from Hardee's. Somewhere inside him he rocks out
to "Billie Jean." I'm too weak to make it all the way, so we stop,
call 911, and wait for the EMTs in the cold-front bluster. All this
rough handling to say, *You who are monstrous are not monstrous, you
are not monstrous.*

BUT THIS WAS SUPPOSED TO BE ABOUT PRAYER and not so much
about getting over a breakup. Let me start again:

IN GRANADA, SPAIN, WITH A FEW FRIENDS, including the friend
from Paris who'd made the tenderest film of faces, I toured the
magnificent Alhambra palace. For hours we were looking up,
photographing the fountains and arabesques and alcoves and all
manner of tessellation. I learned how the fortress flourished under the Nasrid emirs in the thirteenth and fourteenth centuries,
tirelessly expanded with mostly slave labor. Then, in the decline
of the Nasrid dynasty and Islamic rule in Andalusia, the palace
fell to Christian conquest in the fifteenth century with upgrades
in Renaissance style. Then, for hundreds of years, the buildings
fell into disrepair and to vandals, and there were squatters. In the
early 1800s it was occupied by Napoleon's army, who destroyed
eight of the towers with dynamite on their way out, as if for spite.
Soon after Napoleon's defeat, the British rediscovered what was
left of the complex and restored it to a major tourist site. We paid
our admission, we strolled through walls carved in sinuous Arabic
phrases about victors and God.

I KEPT THINKING, IN PARTICULAR, of the squatters in the palace.
Laying down their bedroll and stick fire, falling asleep under tiled

stars, bellies rumbling. Here in the place of the king and queen and sultan and emir, of the French soldier skittish and the vandal eager. And on one of the courtyard stones, I photographed a gull feather and was seeing feathers everywhere because that's what our bodies are in the end, so impotent and fine and lost. In the end, all the same bodies, nobodies. I pictured one of the squatters who died there among the palace gardens the Moors had planted with roses and oranges and myrtle, nightingales in the trees, water trickling everywhere and without proper channel before things were all restored. I pictured his body becoming the white gull feather I photographed on the smooth stones.

A FEATHER COMING LOOSE FROM A WING, left to go dingy, matted, useless, and free.

RIGHT NOW, I PICTURE A few people from the squatter camp at his deathbed pallet, coming around his feather-body and leaving gifts, maybe a sprig of something, maybe a hair comb, a song sheet, and as if all that giving calls up a wind, he simply blows away in the gust into the arcade as they watch. That feather, in all its softness and impotence, will land in puddles, on the dog's nose fluff-barking after a dream-rabbit. It will slip under the couch then blow up onto the belly of one lying back, and on the lower spine of one prostrate in need, or in lovemaking.

THE FEATHER, LIKE ETTY'S PROFUSE and delicate blossoms, offers itself as a blessing, which, in the end, as far as prayers go, is really the kind of prayer I'm talking about: ineffectual beautiful songlike blessing that can fix nothing, slight and inobtrusive enough to slip through the cracks of your terror and grief. Blessings do not lead you out but lead you in. They are clearer than my muddy mind, better than my pettiness. They come at random and trail off like doggerel, though I will sew some together in a small book with this old Husqvarna sewing machine someone gave me. More like a leaflet, little fascicle.

MAY THE LORD BLESS YOU AND KEEP YOU, the Lord's face shine upon you; may you braid back the hair of the girl who asks you to; may your lips brush other lips in an almost-kiss; when the chickens are gone, may you sow the coop in arugula; may the fogged-in mountain roads thread through your apocalyptic dreams and the cornbread and beans round your belly; may you always give away the thing you love most, like the dollar-store bracelet, or a picture of the sea; may there be a fresh-basil smell you can lie down in, under the Japanese lanterns; may wild bergamot grow right outside your door; may you always hear the lambs call out on your way home; may you move on from the roundoff back handspring to another routine, maybe with your baton in the street, twirling and tossing it higher and higher each time and, each time, receiving it back as a gift and a gift and a gift.

BLESSING FOR THE LICE CHECK

MISS ROSIER, WHO WAS CHILDLESS, had us bow our heads to our fifth-grade desks on the appointed day, as though for prayer. She slowly ran the side of a pencil from the nape of each neck to the top of each head. We tried not to shiver as the pencil slipped slowly up our skulls. And if, later, a name was called over the intercom, we knew they had it. They'd be shaved bald; they'd sit alone, smelling of lime and chemical, on the school bus that cut through our small mountain town to deliver us home. Once, a girl was called and she quietly left the classroom with her jacket tied around her waist, her fate sealed. But I found out later she didn't have lice, only needed a maxi pad from the school nurse because she'd gotten her first period, and I didn't see why she had to be called over the intercom as though it were cause for alarm. I didn't see why there couldn't be a cute closet for Kotex in each classroom, amply supplied for shame-free access. I didn't see why, when my friend told me years later, it was unlawful to buy tampons with food stamps, though she said a woman named Lena who owned a corner store by the tracks had let her get away with it.

My friend and I, perhaps because of these specific memories, always get on board for the tampon drive at the Parish House. The boy at the Walmart register must think I'm hemorrhaging as he scans my packages of Always and Tampax. *Look at this blue and pink arsenal,* I want to say to him. *Think of the semiotics of femi-*

nine hygiene products, their shifting meanings. A tampon can signify relief, after that one unprotected night, and, later, grief, the child you wanted once again not materializing. Maybe your childlessness takes your breath in the middle of the night as you overspill your pad and bleed onto the sheets and learn a new shame and hold up your useless hands, like iridescent frog hands outspread in the dark, thinking: For whom will these hands, like my mother's hands, disappear into the bread bowl and reappear, kneading the punched-down dough, knuckles flaked in flour even though wiped on the tea towel before it covers the bowl? For whom will these hands, like my mother's, fold pepperoni into pinched-off segments of store-bought dough, and brush the hot hair away from a face to reveal—out there—the river, the bend, the mist filtering off it, the cobble bar and stones to be held in little hands, and this—the tail feather of a heron? Whose small body will I bathe as my mother bathed mine and filled the Pizza Hut cup to spill over my sudsy hair? But the body, the hands, all shift in meaning, too, since today my mother, in the absence of children, bathes her mother with hospice hands in an atmosphere of multiplied life, years hanging spectral in wavery scenes. Though we don't discuss it, I suppose soon my mother will not have a mother, but is that fully true? Will she be motherless in the same way I am childless, the absence of loss no different from that of unrealized life? Are these even the right questions, since my mother's hands will only and always find another to touch and bathe and wipe the hot hair from so the remarkable river mist smoking off the box elders is in full view?

We cannot be less than we are, less a mother, less a child—but maybe we can be more than we are named. And if our hands reach to touch and do touch, so gently, another, it's as if a new meaning congeals with each moment of contact, a new nameless form of relation fused between two that were once strangers, as even my mother and I once were, at the very start. In this, I begin to see a way opening before us.

Come to think of it, how could I have said my fifth-grade teacher, Miss Rosier, was childless when, during the mandatory check, I felt her hand at my neck parting my long hair as though parting fine feathers, sifting through the strands with the dull pencil lead for any sign of tiny white parasite, each soft stroke of the pencil like a blessing whispered over me—me, her child, knowing her mercies?

BLESS THE SMALLEST HOLLOW: ON LONGING & ONLINE DATING

TED* IS A NINETY-TWO PERCENT MATCH. We both mention Nick Cave, IPA, dismay over webinars. We both write our profiles with enough syntactical variation to suggest a writing habit and with enough tongue-in-cheek to balance the sincere. We answer a third of the dating site's twelve hundred or so questions, lamenting at times, in the add-an-explanation box, the lack of nuance in the phrasing. You can offer your thoughts on pubic hair preferences, littering, humanity's primatial ancestry, meaningless sex. Ted has noted his favorite cuddle position and his views on gun control, Trump, and capitalism. I can sense his deal-breakers. I know his preference for a first date activity and whether he is likely to make me breakfast and maybe take me to Greece.

What I wish the matching algorithms could do is telescope into the nonvirtual and give us side-by-side bodies, while also adding an accumulation of the next several years, to reveal to me, in the future graying and sagging and thickening, what our online profiles portend. Whether he would hold my hand if I were dying of cancer in a white hospital gown with no hair, and whether the gown's white would make him think of the Charolais calf, all

---

The names from OKCupid profiles have all been changed in this essay, and the profiles described here are composites, with some details invented, to maintain individuals' privacy.

snowy and silvery, raised on his family farm for a slaughter he disbelieved because it was too horrible to think real, and whether this would make him think of that Andrew Wyeth painting of the bull calf against the fence wall, and how Wyeth's whites have black in them, have textured shadow and a melancholy, like that white of the curtain he painted with the wind billowing it, how Wyeth tried to paint wind as it crossed yellow-green fields, and somehow tried to paint longing, too, such that Ted would intuit in the folds of the many-times-bleached hospital gown some kind of thing he had never known he'd longed for, welling up through time like a bubble from a gaseous fissure on the seafloor of him—and would he turn and tell it to me?

Ted is a Taurus, like me. Drinks socially, likes Tarantino always and dirty jokes only occasionally. He never litters. He lets those with one item go ahead of him at the grocery checkout. He prefers no drama. He prefers that my drama be so minimal that it fit in a plane's overhead bin. Does not have kids but might want them. Has cats. The most private thing he's willing to admit is that he once took the Love Languages test, though he is not willing to divulge the language he speaks.

A YOUNG BOY HUNTS WITH HIS FATHER AND A GUIDE AND SEES A HAWK. The boy loves the bird's *dazzling speed and the effect of alternation of its wings, as if it were flying by a kind of oaring motion.* It missiles into the trees, he asks what it is, the guide says it's *a blue dollar hawk.* The boy feeds on the name that is almost so fully what the bird is, the boy is filled with the wonder of it, and filled even more so with his newly known hunger for it, as the light of the hawk's being shines through the small tear made in the veil by the guide's naming. Later, in private, the father says, no, that is incorrect, it's *a blue darter hawk,* which is of course right. It's an accurate description of the bird's behavior, and the boy does not feed because the hunger no longer gnaws.

When Walker Percy recounts this moment from his boyhood in his essay "Metaphor as Mistake," he names the hunger an ontological one. He asks, *Is it the function of metaphor merely to diminish tension, or is it a discoverer of being?* Does it satisfy or create desire? Can a metaphor awaken a longing you did not know you had, to bring you the unnameable you were not aware you were trying to name?

I would like to know the origin of desire—the kind of desire that is not prefab, hackneyed, or sold—and so I start reading Avivah Gottlieb Zornberg's book *The Beginning of Desire* about the Book of Genesis, in which she mentions George Steiner's bit in *Real Presences* regarding the paradox of art: art is, on the one hand, *strangeness attenuated*, strangeness made intelligible, its tension diminished, and yet, on the other hand, art—like Percy's beautifully wrong metaphors—also *makes strangeness in certain respects stranger*. So, art slakes our thirst, but it also creates a new thirst.

And there is a space between thirst and slaking, hunger and being filled.

It is a not-yet space in which desire can ripen and you can get to know it.

It is a fertile space.

THERE WERE SOME PSALMISTS WHO ASKED NOT FOR VENGEANCE, not for wealth or throne or relief from leprosy, but only to dwell in the house of the Lord all the days of their lives. Head against the mossy wood of the tabernacle frame, the cool of it, open-mouthed: *One thing have I asked, that will I seek after, to gaze upon the beauty of the Lord and to inquire in his temple.* To live always in the inquiry and not the answer. It's like asking for the roundness of hunger itself as you watch the light hit the acacia beam then travel slowly across the lichen, so slowly across the linen veil's blue and scarlet yarn with which somebody has sewn angels in refrain, a pattern of them.

UNTIL TWO MONTHS AGO, ON my morning walks, I passed by two baying hounds that rightly belonged to a great heath, to impressive hunts for roe deer or wild boar, but who lived in a dinky backyard behind chain-link, crowded by a trampoline never jumped on. The dogs wore running paths that destroyed the grass, their big fleshy ears flapping discordantly with their bodies so taut and aerodynamic. I did not know the breed. Sometimes straw was strewn, presumably over grass seed, in halfhearted attempts to rehabilitate the yard. As I walked past, their big voices sounded their beautiful alarms, like sirens with mournful tones, their longing far too big for their confinement. The neighbors' patience was surely strained, but I loved to walk by them, to hear those deep wakeful tones that said *fox* or *squirrel* or *rabbit* or *woman-shaped foe*, that sang the whole houndbody as braced with want. Hearts so set on having that tiny assemblage of flesh-fur-bone in the mouth—that chipmunk up there—that they would die for lack of it and so up curdled the howl, which was itself a thing and not only an indicator of a thing, perhaps in the way I'm learning that the hieroglyph, though it can be a phonetic sound, is in some instances the thing itself: the owl in its staid glory and not simply the letter *m* the owl represents.

I listened all the way down the alley that borders backyards to the baying that said *may it be otherwise, may it be now, may it be thus.*

They're gone now. No doubt the neighbors are relieved. The grass is growing back. The silence, as I walk by, is palpable.

AT FIVE A.M. I WAS WOKEN BY A DREAM OF A BOY I SHOULD HAVE LOVED. We got coffee once, in our twenties, and parted uncertainly at the street corner. He always tucked in his shirt until he didn't, kept his sandy hair cropped neatly until he didn't. One of four kids, like me, from a God-loving farm family in Minnesota, his heart the size of Minnesota. He went to India, he preaches now,

I think; Facebook would tell me if I were to sign up, would satisfy that curiosity. We spoke in the kitchen where there were mice in the bread bag, with only the stove light on, his skin pale, his cheeks red from kitchen heat. We wrote letters for a few years. By all rights, I should have loved him, but I was young, early in the process of getting acquainted with desire. His letters were penned neatly on the backs of once-used paper—his touch on the world, his press, that gentle and light. I could never tell what he longed for.

WE ARE ANIMATED BY DESIRE THE WAY CONSONANTS ARE ANIMATED BY VOWELS. The Egyptologist Susan Brind Morrow says the vowels in hieroglyphs are not written, so you must sniff out the intent and lift and examine the leafiness of context: *The vowels, which pattern clusters of hard consonants into nouns and adjectives and verbs, are left out, leaving the consonants to stand for the word. Yet grammar resides in the vowels. Why are the vowels not written down?*

Who has seen the wind?

You must get inside the house of a word and feel the breeze blow through. Vowels are the longing of the word. Vowels are the becoming. And so are we defined by the unwritten, the unpossessed, by this that we want which we did not know we wanted because it is unseen, it is unpainted even when painted, somehow secretly seeded in us.

Something in you is activated, vowels breathed into your hard, bony consonants.

THERE IS SPACE BETWEEN GUS AND ME. Gus is the tiny gray stray whom I really should evict. Gus hungry and mewing and snug to the hot water pipes under the house when it's nine below. In subzero intimacy, Gus and me, except not, because I am allergic to cats (I need to break this news to Ted in my next OKCupid message) and because eventually the cat-shit smell in the crawlspace will be pronounced and my landlady will not abide it.

I was not looking for a stray to feed. He just showed up.

"You've been chosen," said my friend.

On my way to feed and water Gus, I pass my landlady's cheesy lawn-decor stone angel with its cupped hands broken off. I've kept it as a metaphor on the patio by the Weber grill left out in all weather, this decorative angel still trying to make (or receive) her offering, even with no hands. I have never liked cats, but somehow my heart stings for Gus like a cut unbandaided in cold air. His right eye a little drippy, I should get him shots, neutered, get a carrier to the vet. His nose presses to my knuckle for a brief nose-kiss, then he scurries under the house. He is a fraidy-cat.

"Well, you can be overwhelming," says my friend.

I worry Gus is undersized and maybe the protein level is not adequate in the food I bought. He is probably picked on by the fat bully cat next door. I really need to call the pet rescue people, I'm allergic, this is not my house, he must go. I have the number on a Post-It but I keep stacking papers on top of it. I picture him in the carrier, looking at me through the cage mesh, betrayed, both of us baffled by this turn of events.

I put out food, break the ice in the water, replace it with warm water hoping it won't freeze so fast. I fish out a plush throw from the blanket chest and stuff it into the crawlspace, mostly impeding his passage, and it soaks in the snow and rain, and I eventually drag it out and throw it away. I offer another of the three tiny stuffed mice from Walmart's pet aisle, twist-tied to the square of cardboard: Skitter Critters, catnips for stimulation, which is *1 of your cat's 10 needs*, the cardboard says, and now I worry about the other nine needs I'm not meeting. Gus's voice a tiny essay of need.

Back at the laptop, I see they call them *essays*, the categories for filling out your profile on the dating site: what I'm doing with my life, what I think about, who I am in summary, which movies I rewatch. The weather hits a warm patch. I complete my essays with the window cracked to let in the night air through the screen, along with the sound of the neighbor's tied-up dog, Perky, whose life is sad and circumscribed, and some answering sounds from Gus whose entry-hole to the crawlspace is directly under my study's window. The cheap curtains from Target billow in the space between us. *Voile*, the curtain fabric is called, the fabric of veils.

I worry about Gus. I worry, too, about Joe who taps the star that says he likes me and who poses unsmiling and shirtless with his ATV in his profile photo, also Rick in a selfie in poor lighting in the bathroom mirror with his shirt peeled up as if to have his abs assessed. I worry for Ed who berates himself for having nothing to *essay* about himself except he is *laid back, not much else to say*, and I wonder what on earth it would feel like to be laid back, also for WyldLover who messages me: *Dam your cute*, and then my worry circles around to Ted who can spell and manage punctuation but can't manage much else, it turns out, is on half a Xanax daily now and, really, though I seem nice, he needs to regroup, he's going on a meditation retreat and disabling his account for a while. I worry for Shelby whose handle is LonelyGuy and Malik (OKCupidLifer), both of whom I want to give a quart jar of soup. I know it seems suspect, or insincere, this concern for the wellbeing of complete strangers, but dating sites expose one's underbelly such that one cannot help but be more attuned to the awful vulnerability of everyone roped into the whole enterprise. The worry becomes a hum that keeps me awake at night.

Wanna fuck? messages Philip from one town over, and, no, I don't really, but I want something that I can't even name and I start to feel as unable to receive it as the handless stone angel, though I do think I'm trying. I shut off the site's app on my phone and carry the picture of Philip for some distance inside my head until he is free of the sports franchise attire and free of the large car against which he flattens his butt and free of, and prior to, the forty-six years of all of whatever, until he is back to his tender small newborn body when there is seeded in him something that will eventually lead him here to this epoch of screens when he will message with an impressively concise, if crude, attempt at a translation of the language of desire. In my sleepless head, he is an infant so small and flailing, so not-yet, and I think of him maybe like my friend's baby: maybe he, too, was born three months early and cupped in the palms of the NICU nurse, his skin so thin it could hardly hold in the zooming blood, all the world's heat and light so feelable yet incomprehensible to his heart the size of a hickory nut. And the nurse maybe said, "You will live. This will be a heart to hold a whole lot." She wiped the yellow film from his face, suctioned out the mucus with the bulb from his pinhole nostril. She said, "All the machines and tubing, all the externalized respiratory system, you will shed. Live into your shipwreck, little one, into all your fierce desire, you'll find your way, bless you, you will be all right."

THE SCIENTIFIC COMMUNITY, LAST TIME I checked *Scientific American*, finds the claims of algorithmic pre-screening for a unique and lasting match bogus. Still, Match.com has over two million paid subscribers. I myself authorized PayPal to pay $15.95 to OKCupid for one month on the A-list. We the people have bought in, and matching has proved easy to monetize. The match percentages quantify toward a goal of satisfaction and fit. And although the metrics do apparently account for the "opposites attract" adage by gauging compatibility as a blend of both similarity and complementarity (the measure of opposite values), I learn that there are sites that narrow options to very specific samenesses: to redheads only, farmers only, tall folks, kinky folks, Ivy Leaguers, Trekkies, whatever your criterion. I learn you can become a Vice President of Matching. I learn the algorithms themselves get smarter the more you use the site; they are "learning algorithms" that are learning you, your preferences and your potential; they can advise you on proper cropping of a photo to attract the kind of person they know you seek based on how you tap Pass or Like, swipe left or right across faces.

And there are so many faces.

Well, images of faces, not faces. I'm taken back to the eagerness of my junior year at university, when I first read Walker Percy and, in a contemporary poetry class, read Ezra Pound for the first time, his "In a Station of the Metro." The two-liner about faces in a crowd, but not faces; instead, *the apparition* of faces, unreal ghosts never becoming faces but instead transfigured into metaphor in the second line: *Petals on a wet, black bough.* I shivered in my desk reading that, I fed on it, made newly hungry. I stored it until twenty years later I would log onto a dating site, recognizing something unnameable Pound was trying to name. Here are the petal-faces you pass on or like, selfies which are ghosts of selves, faces appearing up out of torsos of camouflage beside the eight-point buck just shot.

Alan has kind eyes. I tap Like, and in the tiny rectangle that then appears for messaging I ask, *What is your favorite thing about Richmond?* when what I mean to say is, *I am up at five a.m. inexplicably, after a dream of love for a boy in Minnesota that was not love and the latent regret fills the dark, it's still dark, it's still raining, the rain in the dark is gentler somehow. Also, Alan, I don't know what to do about Gus.*

Thanks for reaching out, messages Alan, which puts in my mind Gus's reaching paw batting the azalea leaves. *I see we both like the outdoors and travel. Richmond is nice,* which does not answer my actual question. I see he has posted a photo of himself hiking in the Sierras, attesting to the fitness of the body, fitness for this, a fit for me. I have posted one of myself, though blurry, hiking with a daypack in New Mexico—See? See how I have caught myself in a moment when I have maybe been beautiful? Do you think? Don't pass on me. Alan's kind eyes appraise me. I notice in his profile he is looking for a woman who is laid-back.

Scientific American cites studies that suggest we aren't very good at predicting what will even attract us to someone, despite our honed search criteria and checked filters all saying: I'm seeking someone of this gender and this age range, located within this mileage radius, with these personality traits, with this education level and body type. Someone who is not messy, is okay with sex in the first month of acquaintance, prefers to split the bill, believes climate change is real.

(What if, like art, love makes strangeness in certain respects stranger? What if our percentage match—yours and mine—is off-the-charts low and your strangeness is out there like a citadel, unconquerable, and I pitch my canvas tent outside you—you, my other—and I curve toward your strangeness like a nervous cat watching your graying face and greening heart?)

Also, studies show the principles of similarity and complementarity can't predict long-term relationship potential like the sites claim they can. And, well, neither can getting a drink at a bar with someone, but bars don't promise you any match predictors, and at least at a bar—at a chance meeting, unengineered—you chafe against the person and hear his skin and hair move, and he's not in an isolated test tube of self, a set of ones and zeros glowed onto your phone screen.

My friend told me users can submit match questions to OK-Cupid, and maybe they don't vet them very well and that's why some of the questions lack nuance. I don't know how one submits a question; perhaps they email the Vice President of Matching.

Dear Vice President, I would like to submit: What will you do if I get cancer? If my spine snaps? What do you do with a word like *beloved*? Why can I not be more laid-back? Why can I not stow my drama in an overhead bin that has that little door which the graceful flight attendant can click shut with the very sound of satisfaction?

What I'm trying to say is, the algorithms offer us a match that satisfies our criteria, but is it satisfaction we really want?

What I love about that Walker Percy essay, "Metaphor as Mistake", is how he confronts us with a choice of two paths regarding our *cognitive orientation in the world: either we are trafficking in psychological satisfactions or we are dealing with that unique joy which marks man's ordainment to being and the knowing of it.* The knowing of it—of being. That you have to get to know it, which takes time. That when we mistake our longing for a lesser thing than it could be, we will, in the end, miss the point.

THIS YEAR, 2018, THE UK HAS APPOINTED a Minister for Loneliness because epidemiological studies show that loneliness is lethal, connected to heart disease, diabetes, and so forth. Like the Vice President of Matching, this appointment is part of a new career field in management of the heart. More folks than ever live alone, or estranged, on this planet, not as often in familial heaps and clans that talk over one another across tables of sausage and potatoes, as we used to live. We're more mobile, less rooted. We age alone, we touch our own throats, feeling them clammy with lack of contact. We are migrant, fugitive populations who don't speak the dominant language, and we are people who live virtually in our bright screens.

And yet, though I'm not sure how one gets in touch: Dear Minister for Loneliness, I would like to submit: While I am in favor of the commission on loneliness because loneliness can kill and can hurt worse than biting aluminum foil, or than a hornet stinging a thud of poison inside your ear (unbearable), and we need to help each other not die from it, I do ask that the Minister take care with the nuances. We need the finest of distinctions, for loneliness can have as its birth-nest real longing, and longing that doesn't destroy you can feed you. The Minister will note that although loneliness is not so good, loneliness as born of longing is essential and more than something to be ameliorated. That we might preserve the smallest hollow. What I'm trying to say is, there is something about that smallest hollow.

———

THAT IS: IS DESIRE ITSELF A FULLNESS? Or at least, is the space between the desire and the having more than empty space to be hurried through like a bad bit of interstate?

Think of it, landscape-wise, as perhaps something more extreme than the swampy drab plains flanking I-75—think of it as a deep and sudden canyon. Real and opened-out. Such that you sleep in the car like the desirous Georgia O'Keeffe so you can wake with such expectation, to paint the stages of the sunrise above the land-gash, with an eye only for the living colors, everything in terms of ochre, verdant green, vermillion. You don't even know where these colors come from. You can't speak. No words beyond *indigo, rose.* All language pictorial and potent.

I HEAR THIS VOICE SAY, For what have you come to the temple? I cannot say, my Lord, my Other. To inquire maybe, with my head upon the acacia beam? Here is this chalice, this hat with a feather, a flask in my satchel, a handwritten prayer in a tongue I can't decipher or speak, in characters of hieroglyphic owl, bread, peregrine. Also, a map misfolded. Isn't it true that if I give all these to you, I will get what I want? Will you fill up my chalice? Isn't that how it works?

Well.

THERE'S THIS LINE SPOKEN LIKE PROPHECY by the roving narrator of Marilynne Robinson's novel, *Housekeeping. For to wish for a hand on one's hair is all but to feel it.*

The longing is a thing, is itself fertile, is not merely a preface for satisfaction. In apophatic prayer, for instance, one creates a hollow and does not fill it. *Silence is not just a precondition for the revelation*, writes the priest Cynthia Bourgeault in her book on the topic. *Silence is not a backdrop for form, and diffuse, open awareness is not an empty chalice waiting to be filled with specific insights and directives. It is its own kind of perceptivity, its own kind of communion.*

And when Robinson's dear, waify Ruthie is left alone on the island by her Aunt Sylvie, the narrator taps Ruth's young-girl desire: *For need can blossom into all the compensations it requires. To crave and to have are as like as a thing and its shadow. For when does a berry break upon the tongue as sweetly as when one longs to taste it, and when is the taste refracted into so many hues and savors of ripeness and earth, and when do our senses know any thing so utterly as when we lack it? And here again is a foreshadowing—the world will be made whole. For to wish for a hand on one's hair is all but to feel it. So whatever we may lose, very craving gives it back to us again. Though we dream and hardly know it, longing, like an angel, fosters us, smooths our hair, and brings us wild strawberries.*

I think of that. Longing putting a hand on my hair. I can kind of sense it now, like my mother's braiding. And a one-time lover lifting my long hair from my throat, pushing it away, like a heavy curtain. This is memory but not only: it is also the round wakeful now. *For to wish for a hand on one's hair is all but to feel it.*

Longing is the angel-girl at the salon. I went to a salon this time, in the next town over, instead of the hair cuttery inside Walmart where I always go, not because the Walmart stylist does a poor job, she's very good, but because at the salon they lay your head back and wash your hair in lemon sage and tea tree oil. And when the young stylist did so I almost broke out into tears at her touch, and the girl said she was bound for Tampa soon, has an apartment with a friend on the Gulf, and she is so ready to go, to get out of her hometown for the very first time. And because she, too, was brimming with want, she probably would have understood, had I let myself cry.

I'm TRYING TO TALK ABOUT THE PAUSE THAT IS NOT A PAUCITY, the silence that is not empty, the ache that is not only.

———

THE NIGHT, OF COURSE, IS THE MOST DIFFICULT. The body is lain out, corpse-ish. The hand moves to the throat touching the accumulative untouch. The skin is never as young as it used to be but is still young. Even so, at times, this thing can happen: it becomes enough to simply lie awake in the dark and not tear in even the slightest way at the fabric of the human community, of another fragile person also lying in state. To, in fact, do more than *not* tear. To even mend, to sew the fabric back together, and to sew it with stars.

I read in Susan Brind Morrow's book of translations of the Pyramid Texts that as a young student of Egyptology she copied out earlier translations for practice, and there was this:

Sew emerald, turquoise, malachite stars
And grow green, green as a living reed

Written on the pyramid wall by somebody fluent in hieroglyphs, in our original writing which must somehow offer a key to our original desire. I copy out what she copied out.

Where, I wonder, does one get malachite with which to embroider? Emerald, turquoise, a yarn hued with the three greenest gems in the earth's crust? That's the thing. But then I think: maybe longing is generative. Maybe the source of such living color is longing itself transmuted. (Everyone knows it can also be transmuted to a lethal bitter black.) And you sew the stars all tessellated, in refrain, lovely like terracotta bath tiles in Marrakesh, ornately, extravagantly, painstakingly. This is a kind of prayer you make when you lie there and worry and weep a little. Out of you the colors come, as fluently as do your tears and entreaties, as if you're a silkworm, and you work, one by one, through the torn-apart, delicate people from your day. You sew them up with star patterns as you sleep alone with the tick of streetlight slanting in through the blinds and the tied-up neighbor dog in her complaint, the room so still but for your hands sewing. Try to believe it's possible, as dawn pinks up, that you might grow into a living reed, a green that is pungent and bright.

I WAS STUDYING THE WALLACE STEVENS POEM "Notes toward a Supreme Fiction," written in 1942, around the time God died. This was Stevens's epoch. This is mine: online dating and almost-weeping in the hair salon, mostly forgetting that God is supposed to have died, thinking God probably lives in the internet. The poet names Phoebus, a god dead like the others, though *Phoebus was / A name for something that never could be named.*

Also:

There was a muddy center before we breathed.

There was a myth before the myth began,

Venerable and articulate and complete.

I think Stevens was looking for the desire before the desire. He wrote: *not to have is the beginning of desire.* The line that gives Zornberg the title for her thick book of reflections on Genesis.

Maybe the myth before the myth began with God the con-cave, God who longs as we do. That is one idea that could have birthed one version of the revelation: that God moves in secret into the womb, beggar-like, and attaches to the uterine lining so Moth-er Mary's nourishment starts to become skin and bone and hair and heart smaller than a hickory nut. All God does in there is feed and web out toes and fingers and float and feel. God's hunger and feeding are one, simultaneous. Then, once born, that cord which renders hunger and satiation inseparable is cut. Then, for God, as for us, they are forever separate things: there is a space between. An interstice. God is birthed first into longing.

And the great cry that it might be otherwise. The cry is syn-onymous with being.

So, I bless the Lord who longs, blessing being an echo of the original blood. *Bless* comes from the Old English *bletsian, bledsian, to consecrate by a religious rite*, the Proto-Germanic *blodison*, *to hallow with blood*, like on the altars. Maybe the etymological path traces not only to the sacrificial blood, but also to the mother-blood.

Bless you, Lord—you, Other I Cannot Name. In my crumpled dress, my crumple-body of want and fear. On my morning walk past the yard where no hounds howl any longer, one day there is snow, so I hitch up the dress above my boots and I find tracks of bird feet in a curved path that ends under the tree that I know to have red berries of some sort in the warmer months but not now. The tiniest feet in the large swallowing snow, wishing the berries there, under all the stuff. Little and big signs of longing that leads us. Bless.

There was this gap of time on Easter morning in my childhood, between the sunrise service held at church in the darkness, before the sun spilled into the sky and the fast was broken with biscuits and gravy and cantaloupe and buns slathered in cinnamon butter—between that and the full Easter Day in nearly blistering light, when the day was a thing I had—in between was a drink. Was when I knew the daffodils around the large-slab rock down by the road, their heads in droop, could almost drip yellow with the tonnage of winter lifted. I knew without seeing that the dark somehow let them be bright under only the three-thousand-year-old light of the stars (incredible that the ancient light still reached, paw-like, to touch). I was in the house, the rooms dark, already drinking in the daffodils through the window screen—like Alice in Wonderland at tea, with the daffodil cup and saucer: sip then eat the pulpy side—and this seemed to me, even as a kid, better than when I would later go out to cut a dozen for the Easter dinner vase from around the stone slab across which I would stretch out in my purple jumper and not have limbs hang over, not even reach the edges. Holding a handful of stems, remembering how sweet it had been a few hours before, in the not-yet.

———

AFTER HIS TEN-DAY MEDITATION RETREAT, Ted resurfaces, messages me on day eleven. He is less fragile now, he says, but one day at a time. I think we might be friends. I think I will ask him about that Wyeth painting of the white bull calf against the stone fence, whether he knows it. I think I will ask his input on the algorithms and on Gus the Fraidy-Cat, who is less fraidy now and getting problematically bold, rubbing up against my leg with a low-motor purr. The weather has broken to a warm spring-ish sog of rain, the subzero nights a memory, and Gus has been tunneling; the landscaping around the azalea is compromised, the black mulch scattered on the grass, down to the dirt. He wants to walk with me in the morning now, but stays on the perimeter, like strays do, not getting their hopes too high but always hoping, keeping open to the possibility of warm love.

All I'm trying to say in these folios scribbled by my heart is that longing is a sign of the branch bending green and toward. And that there's a loaminess between the having and the not having, and from that fertile ground can come a thing you did not know you so deeply desired, and you will be hard-pressed to name it. Maybe you will write many pages trying to name it, and still it will, in certain respects, only grow stranger.

WHEN THE SPIRIT INTERCEDES
WITH SIGHS UNUTTERABLE

A RUSH IN THE HIGH GRASS as when a storm blows up. All the red clover left wild, and the rye and the sedges. My palms skim the flowering head in litany, *this this this*. I am thinking again of prayer, this time of prayer as seeking by feel, like, with no moon, feeling for that face I last touched in the dark (and his earthy scent I last tasted, his ginger-pungent taste I last climbed, like a scaffold). Perhaps God, like a face, is most beautiful by feel. Forelock, hindleg, great ghastly expanse of wing and fur. Brown bats start their secret sounds to find the bugs I stir from the rye. High-frequency calls echo back the whereabouts of gnat. What about prayer as longing to be found in our stirred frenzy? Wanting God—like bats and toothed whales and some species of shrew—to seek us by ultrasound among the wild muscadine? O let my body take shape like a funnel cloud of gnats. Or—since it is summer and we're out—what if prayer is this hiding spot where I crouch under the boulder overhang, an ingenious cubby I'd rather keep secret for my smooth stones, bird-shaped piece of driftwood, hawk feather, possum skull? How about I make a space for you to shelter here, Holy One, and I bring you cold cornbread from the cast iron? We're in here so near, like meat to its walnut, like flesh to its gamy stink. When I tire of crouching and come back out to the fields, *this always this*, my open hand grazes the tips, dizzies the bugs out from the nubbled inflorescence of grain. The thunder uncurls from the sky. A bat brushes my shoulder—a startle not a scare—and my limbs stop, except they breathe like salamander skin. All of me breathes the moonless air, the whiff of wild grape. Somebody is breathing not beside me but in me, through me, saying something without utterance under my own non-utterance. My hand, once cinched like a drawstring, stretches out and pulses in time with the breath. Prayer as God breathing in and out through my skin and gills and lungs—little web-wing bat at my temple, none of me needing to be found under the moonless sky.

WHAT I WANT YOUR VOICE TO DO

We have been busy accumulating solace.
Make us afraid of how we were.

—Rumi (trans. by Coleman Barks)

THE VOICE IS AN ANIMAL'S SNORT BEFORE ATTACK. That is what it sounds like when I read the story this time, that kind of groan and agitation. A guttural hauling-up, the voice ricochets in multiplied clamor, saying, "Come forth." According to second-century rabbis, the soul must now travel a long way back down the southeastern slope of the mountain, a full day gone free. Each morning, for three days, the soul returned from wherever it is souls go to the tomb in Bethany, obliged to reenter the body if possible, but when it saw the skull finally sink in and face disfigure, jaw held on only by a stubborn strip of linen, the soul finally abandoned the body. Fourth day, though, here it is hooking back because the agitated-animal voice calls Lazarus.

The voice uncrushes the head that was beginning to crush, unblocks the man's nerves, unstiffens his rigor mortis, browns the blued skin. This is not the ethereal misty rise the soul was after—no, it is flaccid cock and coiled chest hair and eyes rewetted, skin smelling like the split white root of skunk cabbage. The soul is sucked back into the familiar embarrassment of flesh, but, upon reentry, it understands something is indeed different, unfamiliar. The head is wrapped in ratty graveclothes the man can now sense, he can now fear the feel of suffocation. His hands try to function, to pull off the rags, but he is tightly bound and now feels the binding. Does it hurt worse, I wonder, in the violent undoing? The shock of air in unputrefied lung, the jolt of the blood's resumed flow of oxygen, red, blue, red, blue, the vein map lit inside the body's living night? Nerves first feel sting and then coolness and damp. And sound—after the ear drum is resensitized to vibration—that voice is a hail of iron nails. The man rises up, shuffling with bound hands and feet back toward the life and breath he'd been shed of. And there's Jesus, his Lord, his friend, groaning for him in a tremendous voice, "Come forth, Lazarus, come out." He scuffles, blind, toward the demand that seems capricious. Toward a voice like a beast's before a charge. *Leave me in peace,* Lazarus thinks, rigid with fear, *please leave me alone.*

BECAUSE I AM TEACHING A CREATIVE WRITING COURSE TO COLLEGE FIRST-YEARS checking off their Aesthetic Expression general-education requirement, I am preparing a lesson on voice. I'm thinking, too, about my patterns in recent marginalia on graduate students' work this semester: *the voice is tinny here, the voice is precious, is tonally off—see how the voice goes a bit flat?* What do I mean when I write these things? That the voice does not act on me like a solvent? That it is inauthentic, unoriginal? It has no kick?

Also on my desk is the gospel narrative of Lazarus I'm rereading, and the local paper. On the front page of the *Post* there's an article about a poetry workshop at a middle school here in West Virginia, about an hour and a half drive from the small college where I teach. A professor from another institution has received a service award for the workshop she gave at West Middle School. How kind, I think, helping them find their voices. To the reporter, she said, "That place is real," referring to the school, I assume. There's a nice picture of her, she has nice hair. The paragraphs underneath her photo neighbor yet another story on our region's opioid epidemic, here in the dismal year of 2017, along with a map showing overdose death rates, and I recognize—because I grew up in the county where West Middle School is—that included in the red crisis map is the school in which this bright little workshop took place. The stories are juxtaposed above the weather for the week.

Probably Italian shoes, I think, a dress from Anthropologie, perhaps a whole closetful of such outfits. What's that look in her eye, like a startle? What did she mean, *That place is real?* Her only comment noted.

It's easy to picture myself there since I played girls' basketball in middle school, against West. I gaze around my memory at the dank gym and think, *Hell yes, it's real.* I remember well the girls from West Middle, the meanest in county basketball. They threw elbows and yanked hair, fouled out without fail. They could scramble but not dribble worth a damn. Same was true of me. I played for Central, in a scratchy burgundy uniform, our gym condemned now for asbestos. I remember the fumbling sexual release of it, pounding down the court in bodies that couldn't quite fill themselves or understand the growth of body hair, sprouting out to feel, like antennae. I could rebound, I was good at man-to-man, girl-to-girl, I could make a layup only with wild luck, and in general I shot two-handed bullets. I can see one of those girls sharply in the matchbox gym, a scrapper who drew a technical foul for flipping off the ref and calling him a cocksucker—she'd found her voice, no problem—sitting the bench and picking her face. She was wiry and violent, all elbow, lots of trash talk, she had a real mouth on her and I remember how I marveled. A voice that grabbed you under the ribs and dug its nails in.

It's easy, too, twenty-five years after my brief blur of athletic glory, to picture myself as that professor, since she and I are not that different really. At my desk in my home office, I imagine myself in the language arts classroom at West where the beleaguered middle school teacher catches up on paperwork, relieved that I'll be taking the room for a while. The classroom is bleak, broken chalk, stale air, inspirational posters with faded mountain climbers. My hair is not as nice as the professor's in the paper, but I bring my worksheets and small serious-looking journals and a sheaf of gel pens as gifts.

That place is real. Maybe I know what she meant. She meant high stakes and thin padding. She meant those kids have it rough, they're poor with junkie parents and no food except free or reduced lunch. Their poems will unearth sentimental pain, written in colorful ink with hearts dotting i's and clenched-teeth faces drawn in the margin: this is what Daddy looks like strung out on Oxy, this is our dog Brucey, this is what my mind sees always in dreams, even when I sleep in different houses. That place is real, *that* place, not *this* one, the cultural commons of those who read optimistic newspaper articles, but that other, that doomed one riding the landslide off the cliff.

In the classroom in which I picture myself, there's a cross breeze between the open ancient windows and the door. But the breeze is yellowed, smoky. I say, "Finding your true voice, let's begin."

A VOICE LIKE THE SHOCK OF SNOW ON THE FACE, ice water or ice wind. In the translation of the gospel narrative I have, Jesus *was deeply moved in spirit* when the sisters of Lazarus—Mary and Martha—wailed in grief. Jesus was *troubled.* But this translation does not do justice to the word *embrimaomai,* a Greek verb of great agitation, suggesting a beast snorting, an angry horse stomping and ready to rush—it was this disturbance out of which the words formed, "Come out, come out," voice like rough hands shaking the lifeless body from its rot. Resurging the blood around the grid of bone and sinew. I imagine such a thing would hurt.

Voice says, "Get up."

Summoned, Lazarus bangs his shins, rubberizes the atrophy of leg muscle. The tomb is darker than dark. It takes a while, this terrorizing of each tendon. The first step of resurrection is being aware of one's recent death. Smelling one's own fading decay and feeling the constriction of the graveclothes. The second step is the understanding, like a light switched on: *I can no longer be what I was, there is no going back—something somehow tectonic moves inside me with a great scraping.*

My mind travels from this first-century story down the long chute of human history to where I sat as a preschooler for a fifteen-minute lesson on a Sunday school flannel board. Lazarus looks the cheery mummy. His baffled face is clear of wrappings, blinking away a nap. His won-over sisters—a lean Martha and plump, rosy Mary—are first in sad face, then in happy; it's a simple replacement on the flannel, the disappeared tears. Jesus, with his white robe and blue sash of solace, is helpful-looking, like a crossing guard. And mute. In our small wooden chairs, we can't see, hear, or touch the coiled-up groan let loose in him, the deep churn of disruption and disorder. We recite our memory verse and receive a star sticker. We can't feel the harrowing demand or the flutter of lips mumbling through reedy layers of cloth, "I can't breathe, I can't breathe." Or sense the soul frantic to get back in time, back *into* time, thinking it had finally gotten free of the befuddlement of living.

IN THE CLASSROOM AT WEST MIDDLE SCHOOL where I have pictured myself as the professor worthy of a service award, I imagine how the kids accept my worksheets, which I have decorated with tasteful clip art. I give instructions. They sit at desks engraved with anarchist signs and penises and sunflowers. They hear in their heads a storm brewing. I direct them to the patterned lines, like paint-by-number, fill-in-the-blanks, based off famous poems, cleverly, like a game of Mad Libs. Their voices roam the room with teeth.

I walk up and down the aisles and take in the adolescent fumes
of the boys. Some make spitballs of the worksheets, some give them
a try, thoughtfully pulling at their new facial hair. The girls chew
the pen caps, nervous, adjust a bra strap. One sleeps, one crosses
her arms and checks out. I stop at the desk of a girl in a princess
T-shirt, skinny-to-nothing jeans like seal skin, big boots that were
once some boy cousin's. She fumes on the page in purple gel and
I read that her name is Mindy. She began by filling in the blanks
but soon abandoned them and she has swirled out into the margin.

"I envy you your voice," I say to her.

"Whatever," Mindy says. Tongues her lip ring.

That place is real because the voices are so authentic. (Maybe
that's what the stylish professor meant.) Mindy's voice, as I imagine it, ranges like a wild dog over the page, it has texture, the girl
has material, authenticity—yes, that must be what it is—raw rasp
in the throat. A voice enfleshing a family system sociologists study
from outside the diorama of Mindy's life while the meek school
counselor does his best. Mindy's voice holds a paper plate at re-
unions, two plates layered together though still drooping under
chili dogs. Mindy's voice has a plainspoken face, defiant eyeliner
but hair unmolested by product. It's part of a clan with houses
sloping into one another so that loneliness is not possible except
that it is. The chaos and cacophony lift off in the girl's poem, the
methadone and strychnine, something on fire, everybody's grandma raising someone else's step-niece, and Mindy's mother is a real
piece of work, but loved like the one lamb out of the ninety-nine.
She has sallow skin tattooed with a horse sagging past recognition,
but Mindy always recognizes the horse and she's writing about it,
moving now into the pages of her new journal: from the zodi-
ac, Momma said, born in the Year of the Horse, the Earth Horse
which is kind and ready to help and be there for me—here, I'll
draw it for you in purple, I want that tattoo to stay clear and not
fade like her others—the sailboat with Dad's name on it, the stu-

pid red lotus. This Momma has hopeless blitzed hair and a rap sheet of poor choices and cheap tops, gifted with the condemnation and love of all. The girl's poem is called, in all caps at the top, "A Piece of Work," what her grandmother always calls Momma, though she loves her like the lost lamb. Mindy is tearing through pages, some of the ink trails off onto the desk. The poem says: *The big earth turns in her heart.* The poem smells of the piece of work's Listerine coating her nicotine assmouth. Failed Momma. But the Horse is kind-hearted and so she's coming back for me, she'll come back from Florida any day now.

THAT PLACE IS REAL, WHEREAS this place is not. (Yes, that is what the pretty professor meant.) This place being the life at this desk I have not quite meant to live. I may have meant to live the one parallel to it, I can almost sense it through the fractures of time, like the labyrinthine years in a Borges story. In my memory, somewhere between my lackluster basketball career and now, I had a voice of storm quivering, didn't I? I have worked up through tenure, up through a marriage and out, with a few books but no children. Last month, I had a weird experience: I could no longer hear my graduate students read their poems and stories aloud. So strange, as if there were cotton in my ears. I considered getting my hearing checked.

What if I would have signed on for an outreach to West Middle the day I stopped hearing my own heartbeat when lying on my side? Too nervous to get my heart checked, I wanted to get out of town. To sign on for something real. Lacan's traumatic real, primordial real, unfissured impossible real outside of language. Žižek's symbolic real, imaginary real, or real real, the sublime, the Absolute. Shock of the real—that's it, the shock. I remember back through gauzy folds in my brain, when I once read philosophy and it read like poetry, when I was twenty-one, when I wrote things in composition books that I thought could literally keep somebody alive, or resuscitate, if they were that far gone.

———

MINDY'S VOICE IN THAT IMAGINED CLASSROOM grabs me under the ribs. In the girl's poem, "A Piece of Work," the family sets up outdoor propane burners, making apple butter, coring and peeling with the radio on, and suddenly everyone goes quiet. Momma, too-tanned from Florida sun, makes an appearance, out of the blue. She walks into the yard all hangdog face, shifts her weight, tugs the short sleeves of her Disney World shirt toward the purple needle marks. There is prodigal-daughter silence, an awkward exchange of looks, then she is handed a paring knife and is reabsorbed into the fold.

On the worksheet, the girl has written all around the fill-in-the-blanks and the clever sentence structures that contain them and onto the wide expanse of the back of the paper, and she has scrawled through the notebook and across most of the surface of the desk—I'm glad the teacher is preoccupied with catch-up. Purple pen storming about, horse-snorting, this Mindy who has found her voice or perhaps never lost it, or has never not known it, fire-eyes following the pen tip. She sounds out, clearly, trying to bring her mother back to life that night, because something happened once the apple butter was sealed in pint jars. Purple-pen voice says: "Come out. Get up, get up, goddammit." Voice pulls on Momma's deadweight wrist—maybe Momma hears. In the classroom aisle by Mindy's desk, I stand there with no other way to describe it except that it's the feel of graveclothes on my mouth, tight and restrictive, newly sensed linen holding on my jaw. My hands reach up to tear at it. I can see that I can't see, I can hear multiplied voice against stone. I can't tell if I'm me, or the better-looking professor, or Momma herself, or somebody else. I think: I haven't heard a voice in so long. I think: My soul is long gone over the southeastern slope, and what if it's called back? What will be different? Everything will be different.

I tell Mindy I'm terrified.

She says, "You should be."

She says, "The big earth turns in your heart and no longer outside it."

IT OCCURS TO ME THAT THE SCRAPPER GIRL on the basketball court of my middle school days could have been Mindy's mother, about my age. The Piece of Work, I mean, the one that drew a technical when she called the ref a cocksucker for blowing the whistle on her charge against the scrawny point guard. Mindy's mom and I pounding baseline to baseline. I was number twenty-five, teased bangs weighting my head to the left with several grams of Aqua Net, pretty substantial thighs, knockoff black high-tops. Hers was a throat lined with cut glass, voice scraping its way out, scraping its way back in when she sucked air. Not me, a mousy voice. I couldn't trash talk if my life depended on it. Even then I wanted a voice that could change things, do things—stop pain, stop war, unseat power, disquiet and disturb, fix something broken, break something that needed breaking. Even then I feared the ineffectual voice and struggled against it. On the court, there was effect, she got results—whistle blown, *outta here!* Benched and grim and glowing.

But, wouldn't you know it, she got back in. Only because the team was so small and someone turned an ankle and they had to have five on the court for the game to go on. So she went back in, glowered, got the ball, faked left then jagged right, slipped out of my reach. She flew down the court toward the basket, whipping her ratty ponytail, the crowd roaring. What if this was all a few years before she got pregnant by the listless high school senior with big plans full of furious nothing? And they drifted south to Miami, wanted better things, got into a scene, left her girl since she'd be better off with her grandma anyway, wouldn't she? This pounding down the court in the matchbox gym would have been before the dreams soured, before she whispered to her daughter about the Year of the Horse (*See?*—tiny Mindy tracing the tattoo's outline and tickling her mom's skin). Before she forgot about it altogether.

I HAVE LIKELY MISIMAGINED. THE professor is simply a nice person and the kids probably wrote some nice poems and went home and showed them to their nice mothers whose bodies' ability to produce their own endorphins never flickered off because the Oxy never took over and made them sweat from lung to vein to pore. The kids were probably a little bored and the professor happy enough with her life.

Could be. I've gotten nowhere with my actual lesson planning. I think about excerpting works of literature with voices that at one time reached into me, turned me inside out, as models, though it's not fair to demand such strength of voice of my graduate students just starting out, of my first-years who are mainly trying to pass chemistry lab and who regret not taking modern dance for their Aesthetic Expression credit.

I think about Rilke's "Archaic Torso of Apollo," that last line as the speaker gazes at the sculpture: *You must change your life*, change as a response, an answer, to that stone torso which bursts before you *like a star*. I always loved the poem's claim about art's efficacy. And I always thought it sounded lovely, the end of that poem. But is it really lovely to have to change your life? To have to let go of all you thought you knew, to be so unmoored? Implicit in real *change* is your hair matted to your face in the rain with no way back inside shelter and solace, with only the unknown way ahead into storm.

I leave the desk for supper and sense that neutral and neutered voices fill my head and clutter my house, not voices that unsettle and range like dogs, ravenous to set change in motion. And my own voice is a squeak. Why?

Bothered, I heat up something in the microwave, use the app on my phone to turn on Kai Ryssdal on NPR's *Marketplace* to get the financial news, which then blurs into *All Things Considered* and newsbytes of the US president's voice, Mr. Trump, like a little-lost-boy voice except that he could nuke someone so it's more like a little-lost-boy voice when the boy is burning field mice in a barrel fire, and then voices to analyze that voice, and, no offense to Kai and the others, but they become voices speaking to hear themselves. It feels as though we all speak upward into isolated glass tubes and not to each other.

I listen and listen, eventually take my glowing screen to bed with me, scrolling through voices that reconfirm what everyone already thinks and knows. It's a whole bright world, there in my smartphone warming my palm like a live heart, except it's made in China. The A6 chip, the circuit boards, the slick touchscreen all manufactured from rare elements from inner Mongolia and cleaned with n-hexane that poisons the bodies of workers that now have nerve damage, muscle atrophy, hypersensitivity to cold, so now they wear insulated clothes because of feeling everything too much, every scratchy movement of the world. Maybe they have supersonic hearing, too: hear every voice. You hear, for instance, all the refugees' voices from Syria, from Myanmar, from South Sudan, like bee swarm, fleeing war all over the world, and you hear bits of singing, too, arias like starbursts. You hear secret praying, agitated praying, you hear your students take tentative stabs at their assignment before they delete and start over with something safer and duller and more familiar. You hear it all gelled into the incisive voice of an imagined middle schooler's poem demanding you get up, all the voices like a singular voice multiplied in ricochet against damp stone and you bolt.

NOBODY EVER TALKS ABOUT WHAT THE SECOND DAY MAY HAVE BEEN LIKE, or the third, Lazarus having now bathed and dressed in other than linen strips in the land of the living. Little tremor in his hand he can't quell. Eating a regular meal Martha fixes, on the bland side. Jesus sits there across the table the day after, before leaving town, eyes like wild oceans, and Lazarus looks away and spills stuff, knocks over cups—excuse me, I'm sorry, I'm sorry—gets up from the table because he can't swallow because the big earth turns in his heart, causing indigestion. There are rumors the chief priests want to kill Lazarus because of the hubbub, and Martha is worried, but that's not what's troubling him.

He leaves hurriedly, still a bit weak in his legs from the days in the tomb, goes out to check the sheep. Their little *baa-baa* voices sound like keening. He remembers what it was like to not remember and then to remember and then to dream forward in time. The wind shifts and, just faintly, he smells his body recomposing. How will he live now? The third step of resurrection—now that you can no longer be what you were—is what? It's as if a coil of extraordinary metal glows in the middle of his chest and shoots lava-spears into his lungs, that's how it feels. There is no solace in it, but solace is not what he needs—there is only this love so big and grinding, like a great turning and groaning disc, or sphere. The sheep pasture is near the road and, in each traveler who passes by, Lazarus can feel the dread, rancor, desire, the sadness like a heavy cloak, bits of joy.

"What was it like?" Mary says quietly, coming up behind him. His softer sister with the round, open face. "What was it like being dead?"

Lazarus turns so the sun dipping toward the southeastern slope pours onto his skin, and he says, "Go back home." He can reach inside the very caverns of his sweet sister and lift out her trepidation. Like an ox yoked, he can bear it onward with her.

"No. Tell me, should I fear it?"

He can still hear the voice tear at the fabric. He can still feel the shock of air in nonquivery lungs requivered. He will never forget that. But even more alarming is the roiling movement in Lazarus's heart, a nuzzle of lamb behind his knee and his soul feeling it like a burn, the golden sun on his face.

He says, "I'm not what I was, but what am I?"

Her eyes like the sheep's. How to begin describing all this to his sister, whose heart now thuds in his own?

THE LIP-RING GIRL. MINDY. *GET up*, she writes. Momma trembles, from something other than the stuff she shot into her vein. Shock of light in her eyes so her pupils respond. There's an awful intake of breath. I tremble, too, I drop things on the classroom floor, the extra pens and worksheets, my bag. Mindy says: Wrestle out of the linen binding, work free the strip that's tight around your jaw. Change out of the fouled clothes your dead body shat in.

What a jolt this is—resurrection. It hurts only at first, but it hurts like hell.

Grope in the dark, to find by feel the tomb's slit and crawl out.

Once out: you think it's sunlight that pierces you, you who were used to the dark, such a burst of it that you shield your eyes. But whatever it is, it's not outside you. It's inside, radiating. It can only be love for the world spinning on its axis behind your ribs, against your kidneys and spleen, the earth throbbing in the beat of your heart.

THE NEXT DAY OF MY REAL LIFE GOES BY. The boy who lives next door to me, Brady, takes off running as fast as he can down our street for no reason and every reason, yelling like crazy. I sit on my front steps so I can hear his joyous, raucous voice. I take a beer out there, and yesterday's lesson-plan notebook. Wave to Brady's mom. In the notebook on my lap I make notes: I want your voice to make me different than how I was. To make a memory of my death. I want mine to do the same for you. To raise the dead. Brady flies, he pumps, his hair doesn't move, it's lodged in beautiful scruff-coil. His limbs are lengthening.

"Hey," I say.

"Hey," he says. Runs on. *Weird woman who lives alone next door.*

Then his dad sets up the hoop in the street since traffic has died down, and Brady pounds the basketball, pound pound pound, he dribbles off his toe. He doesn't pay me much mind on my porch mumbling in my graveclothes, prying them from my face so I can breathe. Kid's as bad as me at layups. Gasp air, fill lungs, feel the big sphere turn and scrape. I cross the street for a pass, one dribble and a jump shot. A hopeless air ball, and we laugh and howl.

BLESSING FOR HOMECOMING

Untouched, I think of salt blocks for deer. Trace minerals and molasses in ten-pound cubes that men around here put out between the whitetails' water source and their bedding in the briers. To lure game, they say. But I know, for some, it's only a kindness. Sometimes, a hunter sits still in the tree stand with no rifle, thermos unlidded. Watches a fawn falter then recover, a mother's rough nudge at the flank, soft mouths hovering at the salt then taking part. Tender version of himself a specter of black coffee steam in the dawn air. Then I think of bucks in velvet, wild buck rub against the sapling in rut season, doe in heat bleating. I need a walk.

It's October, a Saturday evening with cold crisp light. At the river, high schoolers pose in taffeta and tuxes in front of gold-leaf sycamores and broken benches. Must be Homecoming. One pair catches my eye, their two sets of parents ready with cameras. The girl stands under a near-done apple tree and looks cold in capped sleeves. Corsage of a white rose dyed blue on its tips half-rhymes with her frosted blond tips on dark strands unsecured by her French twist. The boy—in matching boutonniere, cummerbund a loose approximation of her yellow chiffon, jacket boxy and big— does not touch her. Inches away, his adolescent body utters something out loud to hers in a frequency only she can hear. These two will not be crowned king and queen. He takes her hand for the last few photos at his mother's request. He takes her arm, of his own volition, and helps her climb the running board of his dad's diesel pickup, and they drive off toward the school gym.

I am with the mothers then, and the sweet rot of the apples fallen to the ground, and the fathers with hands in their jean pockets, not holding their wives. We stand there regarding the high schoolers' heads through the truck's back window, the girl's updo further escaping its bobby pins. The five of us an odd ensemble of witnesses. One of the mothers holds up a hand to wave and holds it there, like a clergyman speaking a blessing. *May the poison ivy rash like raw meat, and the pink calamine lotion smeared over leg stubble you couldn't shave, not show up in the photos. May your cheap shoes bloom no sore on your heel.*

How many years later now, since the man who was once my husband left, do I sometimes recognize in the mirror a self that heard his voice in the other room, like a soft scare of rabbits—his hand stoking the woodstove with a dry stick of pine—and walk through the door expecting him there? Yet this moment just after the photoshoot, in a body unheld, alert in all the October air and standing with these others also separate, each in plaid shirt and unbecoming slacks and sweaters, and one mother thinking how her child once ran home to her voice calling out like a wood thrush— this moment yields a sweetness all its own. As if, alongside the mother with her hand still in midair, I am permitted to bless them. As if, alongside the hunter, I can sit, the hunter who more often takes aim, kills, guts and skins and handles the meat of a buck in full embrace, but who this time only watches the yearling breathe, the stubbled hide of its body so coarse and beautiful a container, and wishes for its life to keep intact for all that will come, for all that is uncontainable. *Taste salt and sweet molasses, little one, bed down in briars too young to be thorned.*

SUNDAY MORNING COMING DOWN

WRITE THE WHOLE PAINTING AND DO NOT STOP. Sunday is bitter cabbage and the glimpse of shapes down a brief hallway, involved and intent shapes. I am more cognizant of breath on Sunday—the way, as bodies lying on our sides like long-legged fetuses, we are aware of the heart whomping in the ear. On Sunday (a day welled up with the week past and the week to come such that you experience all the days at once like a person set down, weary, before a painting), breath feels like the respiration of time, like God's breath. I am losing my morning heat from the down-pocket of bed, enclosing myself in sweaters, but still I cool and require the space heater this day early in Lent. Sunday is breath and chill and stillness, the bitter salted cabbage as I help make the kraut, its tangy smell hazing the hallway.

The directive is to write the whole painting.

R, the man I'm seeing, recently gave a point-of-view craft lecture on whole-painting writing: Give the story all at once as if you're trying to confront someone with an acrylic on the wall—can someone receive a story on all levels, not in narrative sequence, not in sequestered moments of time, not from one point of view but a shifting one? During the lecture a student in the front row *yessed* like a Baptist who has read the Scripture the night before and so already knows the parable, *yes*, how the kingdom of heaven is like a mustard seed that grows into the largest tree in the garden, with all the loud birds roosting there as they might roost in the tree in his chest, so, *yes*, he said while each downbeat syllable of parable fell from the preacher's mouth. Which was the lecturer's mouth, R's mouth, reading excerpts from Lawrence Durrell and Kay Boyle and William Goyen that traversed time and perspective in shock-color layers. Try to write the whole painting, R said, even though we can't ever write the painting, for all we have is language, but, *yes*, the student already knew the struggle that each writer in the room knew, the impossibility, and the insistence that we go forward, marching toward failure, amen and amen.

The directive made me want to write about Sunday.

Perhaps it's because, as a child, Sunday was the day I felt an intersection of currents and a simultaneity of layers. I felt the press of eternity's hand because of the habit of church where all forms and patterns and braiding-back of my hair were intended as poor representations of realities timeless and glorious. The Sunday moment is sharp and prismatic in my mind: stepping a penny loafer down from the Dodge to the gravel, decked out in my mother-made dress with wooden buttons I'd picked out myself at JOANN Fabrics and a jean jacket over top, a cheap silver locket secreted against my chest bone. A lush spring Sunday, all the lilacs slouching wetly. Maybe that childhood storehouse of Sunday strikes brightly now, like red and yellow acrylic, because of today's austere Lenten air, though I don't know that a Sunday in Lent is any different from one in Ordinary Time. It seems, in our cyclical week, Sunday is a measure, a ritual of reckoning, an end, a beginning, full-bodied and populated. Things come to bear on Sunday, things you have borne, how things will bear out. All is with you, all you have loved, hated, vowed to never leave and yet left.

I HATE SUNDAYS, I TELL R. I dread Sundays.

SUNDAY SEATS YOU CLOSE TO A PORTAL. It's very like stomping the cabbage each year for the kraut. A child is engaged in a chore that pins her to the kitchen bench facing the brief hallway of motion and sound. Time moves more slowly here, or more quickly, or both. She turns to see her mother come through that front screen door portal with even more cut cabbages mounding in the granite washbasin propped on her hip, cabbages sliced from the stalks, from among the big-blanket furled leaves. The mother cuts out each core then shreds the cabbages, for a few years, with the manual kraut-cutter that looks like a washboard with blades, like an oversized cheese grater, then, in time, with the electric food processor, in batches. Then she dumps it all into the crock on the floor between the benched girl's knees. The mother salts a layer, dumps another—salt, sift, dump, salt.

I DON'T THINK IT'S LOGICAL, R says, not unkindly—it's just a day like any other. (And it's true that I am sometimes quite illogically unmade on Sunday, in tears and wadded up with my dog on the couch. This is baffling.)

I say, But the past is always with us, like Faulkner said, you like to quote Faulkner, it's like that, the days are always with us, and on Sunday somehow you can feel the days well up.

Dreading two back-to-back seventy-five-minute gen-ed classes is logical, he says, which is why he dreads Tuesdays and Thursdays.

But in a recent email to me he wrote: *Life of course is the whole story at once and our frustrations with it are the tiny boxes we try to force it into. In both writing and life we have weak artificial mediums to work with, words and time.* So he does understand.

Should we have a baby? I say.

What?

I'm nearly thirty-seven, I remind him—my window of time is circumscribed, biological clock and so forth.

So that's what this is about.

Logically, yes.

———

R HAS READ EVERYTHING WILLIAM GOYEN EVER WROTE, has even read the newly released biography. He included in his lecture how Goyen didn't write for self-expression but for the communal voice, in multiple frames, in tales nested in tales, his words and paragraphs stick figures—black letters upon white pages—but flesh hangs from them like jellyfish skin, translucent sheets billowing, flesh and dress ballooning into color and light. Goyen's stories are festooned with other stories, or infested—it's like traveling down someone's throat lined with rubies. This is the Goyen who wrote inside a parenthetical in *House of Breath*—a book in which sentences sometimes don't stop for pages—*who knows the unseen frescoes on the private walls of the skull?* I don't know who knows, but Goyen tried to write them, to catch the brightest color right when the fresco went up on the lime plaster, before it could dry.

IT'S TRUE THE BABY QUESTION TROUBLES ME with a louder clang on Sundays. A baby's tiny skull and heat and light and hair, do I want to try? Lots of women turning thirty-seven this year are fearing they will regret not having children, but is fear reason enough to have them? My friend K writes in a letter, *Is the pang of knowing you will not know the profundity of that kind of love any reason to have a baby?* Out of desire for profundity? K is a friend to whom I often write on Sundays, the practice of a Sunday letter being one of my coping strategies.

Ought I to have a baby, as though it were completely up to me and a matter of my will, like donating to Mothers Against Drunk Driving when they call? And why do we say "window of time"? It makes me think of Madeleine L'Engle's *A Wrinkle in Time*, her lovely powerful Charles Wallace, the little boy ready to travel through time. I remember the word *tesseract* and my brother's science project on black holes, the model he built from a coffee can and a Yahtzee box, aimed just so at the mirror hanging on our parents' wardrobe that held things like our handwritten immunization records and Murphy's Mart bags full of material scraps for quilts Mom would make over the next forty years, preferring to sew them by hand. I suppose we say "window of time" because of the frame of limitation. But what if it's another part of the metaphor's vehicle bearing forth a different tenor, what if it's because of the window glass to see through, to be seen through, like a portal? Like a passage?

Like a hallway of time: what I am talking about is becoming a memory for a child who looks into the passage of time, the memory making an imprint. Back to that same screen door, for instance, portal from indoor to outdoor, the girlchild-me watching her mother who has boiled water for ear corn, now that krautmaking is done, removing the corn then carrying the pot through the screen door that closes with its soft slap upon its spring and tossing the silk-littered water off the side of the porch instead of in the sink, and standing a few beats after, listening to the supper hour shift and adjust. The image of it through the screen mesh in the greening light will be forever recycled in the girl's mind by dream by dozing by grief by time.

So who will see and know me in that way? That is the question to catch in my throat. I am creating no tableaux of oddity and ritual upon a porch floor to wake in the mind of a child after me. I will disappear. I will have to be okay with disappearing. Or try to be recalled another way, and this is maybe why I'm writing a novel in which a woman remembers her mother just so, with the pot in her hands emptied of all but a few corn silks. And if I can write in a way that comes up off the page in translucent sheets of flesh and color, billowing from the letter-bones, like absurd and wondrous jellyfish, like a slow ornate pop-up book, or full-face like a painting all in acrylic of searing brightness—then maybe that is enough. Maybe that is how to spend my window of time.

I wonder, do I sit on a cold Lenten Sunday to simply write against my own disappearing?

To the average American male, R says, Sunday means one thing.

Sex, I say.

No. Professional sports.

Right, I say. R may not understand the dread of Sunday, but my friend A understands. Another fucking Sunday, she says, AFS, we coin, *Happy AFS! Here is a Ziploc of cookies to get you through AFS, I had AFS on Monday this week*—so go our texts and emails in between the classes we teach. *PMS on AFS, double whammy.* She gets the Sunday *New York Times* delivered and reads it all, as palliative. And my friend SB understands. She's in favor of our new acronym, she's Pentecostal after all, she understands the kit of things needed for AFS Survival. Sometimes she goes sailing.

At its most basic, it's the smeary weight of a sinner's penance, or, with the weekend almost over, it's Monday creeping close with its job-gloom. It's the knowledge that Friday's buried memory of failures will be Monday's pert reality, or it's the nostalgic chime of a church bell calling because you once wavered hot like a mirage with the rest of the faithful through the hymns and it's been a while. It's the memory of family time, all the Sunday dinners, and now your siblings flung far across the world calling home on Sunday, if there's time. It's concomitance of vague emotions, sentiments layered together like filo dough.

At its utmost basic, it's the terror of one's annihilation.

Johnny Cash understood, as he understood everything. I sometimes YouTube his hangover song, his cover of Kris Kristofferson's "Sunday Morning Coming Down":

On a Sunday mornin' sidewalk,
I'm wishin', Lord, that I was stoned.

> *'Cause there's somethin' in a Sunday*
> *That makes a body feel alone.*

SUNDAY MORNING COMING DOWN LIKE a fog, a curtain, a crumbling ceiling, an axe.

I LOVE "SUNDAY MORNING, 1950," a poem by Irene McKinney, the way I can slip into the poem's background in my dress with wooden buttons from the 1980s:

> *In the clean sun before the doors,*
> *the flounces and flowered prints,*
> *the naked hands. We bring*
> *what we can—some coins,*
> *our faces.*

I LOVE ROBERT HAYDEN'S POEM "Those Winter Sundays" which I have taught in several classes:

> *Sundays too my father got up early*
> *and put his clothes on in the blueblack cold,*
> *then with cracked hands that ached*
> *from labor in the weekday weather made*
> *banked fires blaze. No one ever thanked him.*

Sundays *too*, in class always emphasizing that tiny adverb that's so heavy, for there was no reprieve for him from the cold that cracked his skin. Fires must be built on Sunday morning too, ashes must be shaken down, it is a day that is no different from any other but it was the day on which he noticed the lack of gratitude. It was the day he was lonely. And the day his son remarked, memorialized, as having a palpable difference.

———

SUNDAY IS THE KRAUT-STOMPING BECAUSE, when you're stomping the salted shredded cabbage with a thick cherry branch shaved and sanded smooth, you watch the patterns in the linoleum and wait. You have a sense that it will be the others' turn at the chore soon, later, long later it seems, because, as you lift your head, they—two brothers and a sister—blur through the short hallway to the bedrooms and bathroom and back out. The space swells with their bodies. They pass by to move through the screen door portal, out to the porch floor, then to circle the house on bikes on the path grooved and grassless. Time swells with their movement and faces and teeth come in crooked and hair curly like the Brillo pad your mom will use to make the floorboards shine, the whole floor, on hands and knees, once all her kids have left, still scrubbing at the years of drifting-down skin cells and dirt. Now you smell the clean foam of the bitter cabbage and foresee the banded linen towel or old pillow slip that will shroud the crock for six months in the basement corner. Six months of waiting under a thick layer of mold and souring, almost rotting.

Stomp-stomp with the sanded stout branch, preparing the salted cabbage for waiting. Waiting too for your life to start, to join the blur of motion. Plunging the kraut stomper between your knees down into the crock untapered, the sound of the screen door slapping shut. There is dread in the waiting, for you feel you will run out of time.

I'M NOT SURE YOU WANT TO HAVE A BABY. He tries to say this not unkindly.

Maybe I'm confusing desire with dread.

IT DOES HELP SOMETIMES TO WRITE LETTERS ON SUNDAY. It's a hopeful stutter of voice sounded before working on the novel. Today I answer my friend J's six dense pages of lovely longhand, all her news about the new rooster—*He is all colors a rooster can be and looks handpainted*—and about Iris the feral cat, and Beloved the horse not yet trained well enough to ride, and J's own blurring eyesight.

Then novel work because part of my survival plan is to write on Sundays all the way through until noon. This time is demarcated on my weekly schedule color-coded with Prismacolor pencils from my childhood desk cubby, pencils that once shaded the eyes of a lamb on a newsprint Easter kite. Why noon, as though something magic shifted at noon? Because it indicates a fully committed morning, to give it everything, everything you remember and half remember and inexplicably love. Beside me hangs a painting— Georgia O'Keeffe's *Cow's Skull with Calico Roses*—a canvas replica I ordered online. I wanted to see the longhorn skull better because the section in the novel in which the character has a conversation with a cow skull was growing more and more confusing. I wanted to see the whole skull before me and I felt it important to get the one she painted with fake flowers as garland, and I felt it important that the skull looked like a womb, shredded down toward the nostrils, like pulverized cabbage. Why, I'm wondering, does my novel's main character miscarry, and why does another character throw her babies away? Why the thwarted womb like a portal, all banded in suffocating gauze? Why not write a mother? I don't know why. I'm writing in half dream, that is all a novel really is.

I LOVE ABRAHAM JOSHUA HESCHEL'S 1951 BOOK *THE SABBATH*. In Judaism, the Sabbath is Saturday and not Sunday morning like it is for the Baptists and Methodists, parking trucks at a slant in ditches beside overfull gravel lots, but the principle of the day of rest, the set-apart holy day, is the same. I remember dressing for Sunday service once and asking my mother, Why do we dress up for Sunday? Because it should be a different day, she said.

Heschel writes about the Sabbath as though it were something we go out to the porch to see in all its loveliness. It's a day released from labor, but *its spirit is a reality we meet rather than an empty span of time which we choose to set aside for comfort or recuperation.* It's *a day on which we are called upon to share in what is eternal in time.* It's *a palace in time which we build.* Time's passage again taking spatial dimension: a stone passageway of ornate carvings and tilework. In the atmosphere of such a palace, Heschel writes, *a discipline is a reminder of adjacency to eternity.* Its discipline and abstentions are what it's known for—and so is the traditional Christian's Sunday Sabbath, never stopping at the grocery store to spend money after worship, never cranking up the Weed Eater. Reading Heschel on my Sunday Sabbath, an icy Sunday during Lent—the very season of abstentions—I feel a strong desire to run out to Go-Mart to buy some peanut M&Ms, just to slip out from under the weight of all that beautiful principle. But I keep reading about Sabbath as a presence, felt and arresting and palatial.

On Sunday I feel the unbearable welling-up of time and see what the kraut-making girl sees: her mother and sister and brothers in a blur of color as she stomp-stomps the crock floor and the abrasion of the tough leaves makes them give way to juices that foam up rabid. What I see from the kitchen bench is my mother's longing, my siblings' movement out into the world, as if the image of that hallway off the kitchen is a breach of time, an image conjured on a day, Sunday, which is a day when time being culled out from eternity is understood as illusion. On Sunday maybe we see for a moment how God sees, without illusion. Maybe we try on the timeless gaze of God and try to breathe and bear it. What a dreadful, awful gift, to lose time's blinders.

There is the story in the Book of Genesis about Hagar, Abram and Sarai's servant turned concubine, turned surrogate. Pregnant with Abram's child, she flees the barren Sarai's jealousy and cruelty.

Out to the wilderness Hagar goes, loosed and flapping in the wind, pregnant with the shifting blood of her boy Ishmael who will be cursed into terror like a wild donkey. She slumps by a spring seeping up from the dust. She is weary, but she is visited, and she calls the spring *Beer-lahai-roi*, Well of the Living One Who Sees Me. I have seen the one who sees me, she says, as though she suddenly understands what it means to be seen by such a gaze as God's. Hagar becomes one of the few to understand what God's gaze takes in: fetus unfurling, woman with a tooth aching at the root, for it's loosening, hair falling out, pelvic bones reconfiguring in the third trimester from marrow to foam rubber, and also her last gasp, her burial, and lilacs thrown upon her grave. The whole painting, all layers at once, every window of time.

It is not really imaginable, that kind of gaze. Even on a reflective, moody day like Sunday, we can feel only the overwhelming layers of our own lives. The past is with us (says R to me, says Faulkner, says the experience of divorce, says the adult body returned home briefly and sleeping in the childhood bed—I remember when it was the four of us, a heap of breathing, anxious and fertile and unstoppered breath, and how our mother's voice now echoes, *Just once more, can it be that way*, as she runs clothes through the wringer and the house thickens up with voicelessness, and she scrubs the floorboards to luminous glow with a Brillo pad). Even just our own lives are unimaginable. Think of all the others—maybe what the girl making kraut sees in the brief hallway is the blur of motion of the others, not only brothers and sister but all the others, the eternal within time, the story nested in story, and the attempt she would one day make to write it down, the whole of it.

I DO NOT KNOW ABOUT A BABY.

Sometimes it's just about wanting what we don't have, R says, and this helps.

I picture my heart opening—how wide it can open if I let it. That wideness is what gratitude is, and I think, on this cold Sunday, that the practice of a Sabbath is a fight for gratitude in the midst of quiet panic, in the face of your window closing or going dark. And gratitude trains our eyes on *what is eternal in time*. It's as if gratitude creates time, lays it the way a hen lays eggs, little minute-chicks open-mouthed when hatched in the nest, and they trill and cry, trying to add sound to the painting, for it should have sound too. Heschel writes about running to the Sabbath with sprigs of myrtle, as if to a bride. Wear your most beautiful robes, sing your most beautiful songs, bring your most beautiful acrylics.

Who knows whether it's true that, in the end, all we have are these minutes and hours to measure our lives, that all we have are these poor marks to work with, black symbols on white pages. It could be that we have everything.

WHEN SEX IS HARD FOR
CHRISTIAN GIRLS

THE MARE GOT OUT. The woman is thinking about getting out too, looking down from the window onto the barn and the unyielding garden. Both in her skin and out of it, in a shift dress, her life heating her up from behind, blowing its hot breath. On the worktable: halved and quartered potatoes for soup, a few measly ones she grabbled out from the failed crop. Beside the starchy cutting board: a yard-sale teacup full of bachelor's buttons floating in water. A jar of tea made from bark with no honey. A tablet of paper from the Dollar General—no lines. Big, still, soundless pages. It seems a lot of people know what they're doing—"I wrote an aubade, it flowed out like song"—not her. Someone said to write something and mail it in for a contest, you get your name in gold on a pen, just a twenty-dollar fee. Sometimes she writes only one word on a page, like labeling the butcher paper of wrapped meat. She wants work she understands. As long as it's work, she understands. She writes *tenderloin* over and over, like a stutter. Just let go, let loose, someone said. She writes *let go, let loose, let by, lay them by.* Like what she does with her potato vines, *lay them by.* Hill up the dirt around the stalks and let the heart-shaped leaves shrivel and give themselves entirely to the unseen Kennebecs below, to fissure them out in tuber and tuber, sometimes twenty to one, in a decent-yield year. Not this year. She did everything right, mounded dirt in the furrows, she doesn't understand. But failure and bounty are no business of hers. She can know only her hand in cool dirt and wants to, now. She goes outside, blown by her life's hot breath. The sky tilts down toward her failure with its harsh blues, and her failure tilts her up toward the sky. There's the horse-barn, froth of aster against it, elm drooping as if wet. The mare is still out. In the distance, real small, the mare runs and is magnificent. Inside the barn, motes snow down on broken bales. *Lay them by*, it's songlike, lay the body by, let it give itself to what is secret. To the goodness of down. Down, she is hided with fine hair visible when the balder light subsides. There may be no stranger find than her own hide felt, found on the cool barn floor. Something lush there, something easy.

BLESSING FOR THE
DEMOLITION DERBY

MAY NO GAS TANK BLOW, no face burn like a lamb shank. May the scrap metal prices come back down to keep crashable cars under a hundred, or at least one fifty. May Jack, with whom your brother is roofing houses this summer as you clerk at the feed store when you are both on break between college terms, make it to the last heat in his Chrysler Imperial, and the loudspeaker speak his name. May your brother cheer—your brother who smells of asphalt and sun beside you in the stands and who, years later, will tell you he doesn't remember going with you to the Friday night derby at the Valley District Fair—watching that first Chevy Impala crumple like a soda can. And if a tank does blow, may it char only one side of the body, mostly arm and thigh, as it happened for the boy from your high school in the Terra Alta derby you did not witness, when he couldn't get the belt unfastened. May the face be chastened but uncooked.

After the Crown Victoria loses a fender in the third heat and they call an intermission so the dust can clear, like a temporary truce in war when both sides could gather their dead at dawn in a strange sad peace to let people hold all that they'd broken—and just before you go check out the concessions, may each dazed man rise slowly from the driver seat to sit in the car door window sheared of its glass with hammer and horsehair brush, taking stock of his damage so far. At first halved, with legs inside the car's crushed metal, may each grow whole as he crawls out of the window so tenderly as if into someone's arms, as if a child gathered up with his hope enormous and his ideas dragging behind him where he toddled the road lined with tractor parts and elderberry. May they emerge this way, like dead bodies resurrected, if indeed bodies get resurrected with all the same tattoos and Skid Row muscle shirts and feathered hair, their skin a shade paler but it's probably just the glaring arena lights. May you remember this brief surreal image however many times in your life you'll need to believe that impossible tenderness in the midst of destruction is what saves us. May you store in your mind this brief surreal image, as you order two snow cones and the revving starts again, so that you may remember this whenever you need to believe that impossible tenderness in the midst of destruction is what saves us.

May the Fire Department chicken dinner still be going on after this is over, and the sky stay clear for the ox roast tomorrow and for the tractor pull and the mud bog and the Tilt-a-Whirl. May one of the menstruating girls outside the Parish House Food and Clothing Bank, with a sweatshirt tied around her waist, waiting in line not for stale pastry, not for a canned good or a garbage bag of clothes with white things pit-stained and pretty things pilled, but for a box of Kotex after there's been a tampon drive—may she win the fair's pageant this year. May the loudspeaker speak her name along with Jack's over the ruckus of metal on metal. And when another Impala gives up its ghost and the blue-raspberry snow cones you got for your brother and yourself turn your tongues blue, so ice-cold they burn, may you drink all the juice pooled in the bottom tip of the cone at the end, the nothing-like-fruit, all indigo dye and corn syrup. May you survey the arena, under the halo of lights, and take in each face through the windshield absent of its glass, faces eerie now and more naked, and linger there till the final heat.

THE STORY OF MARY AND MARTHA TAKING IN A FOSTER GIRL

I STAND OUT HERE, in the blacker air with the night bugs, in need of a new story. My predicament is common enough, standing in the wake of another lover having left for good. Some bafflement, heart in my throat throbbing, that sweet sense of possibility drained. Stuck and narrowed, I need to pull on the natty sweater, light the lantern, and write all night for love's possibility despite the givens. As I often do, I seek the new story in the husk of an old mythic one.

"I remember the day we made the cake," says Mary to Martha in the kitchen. Mary finds Martha crying soundlessly and says, conciliatory, "We made the cake out of nowhere for nothing, it was a lark."

Martha, skinny as a rail, Martha with her spreadsheets and to-do lists and steel wool, shakes her head *no no no*: "I'm not capable of a lark. All I can do is prepare *meat*."

"Remember how you boiled the orange, pulped it with peel and pith and all, and we baked it into the dense chocolate with soppy whipping cream on top?"

"It was soppy because you got sidetracked," Martha cries. "And the white peaks didn't form properly in the bowl."

"The berry atop each slice was your idea. It wasn't even anyone's birthday. And you left the rest for the racoons and crows, remember?"

Mary hugs her sister at the waist, and it's like hugging a fencepost. "All I mean is you made the cake for nothing." She opens her hands as if to say, *Your heart gives, your heart has some give to it.*

THE ORIGINAL STORY-HUSK IS IN THE GOSPEL ACCORDING TO LUKE, chapter ten. In the last five verses, Jesus comes to the village of Bethany, Jesus who wanders, with no itinerary or forewarning of a large party of guests. In the English Standard translation of Luke's Greek, the story goes: *A woman named Martha welcomed him into her house. And she had a sister called Mary, who sat at the Lord's feet and listened to his teaching. But Martha was distracted with much serving. And she went up to him and said, "Lord, do you not care that my sister has left me to serve alone? Tell her then to help me." But the Lord answered her, "Martha, Martha, you are anxious and troubled about many things, but one thing is necessary. Mary has chosen the good portion, which will not be taken away from her."*

And that's it about the sisters. Luke plows right into chapter eleven in which Jesus composes the Lord's Prayer on a hillside and offers an analogy about the givingness of God: If a son asks for bread, will a father give a stone? If a son asks for an egg, will a father give a scorpion? (He does not mention that it would be a woman bringing the bread and egg and meat and cutlery.) And although Mary and Martha show up elsewhere in the Gospels— there's the business of their brother Lazarus being raised from the dead—no other Gospel writer renders this version of the story of Jesus's visit to Bethany. We don't know what happens next for the sisters in this scene.

In Luke's account, Mary is free and open-hearted, sitting and drinking from the font of the Lord's words, refreshed. Martha is sweaty and harried, concerned with appearances and with making an impression, hospitable only transactionally. No one told her there would be so many, she's nose down, powering through to make sure they all eat their fill. She must stay in control, so she is, ultimately, *missing it*. Martha the scold and the nag, alone in her toil. Mary shirks the customary duty of women to serve, which I admire, of course, but Jesus and the men must eat, someone must fill their glasses. So Martha inserts her gaunt face between the Lord and the seemingly idle Mary to say, in no easygoing mood, "Tell her to help me," or, closer to the Greek: "Bid her take a hand along with me in the work." "Martha, Martha, you are worried, upset, careful," says one translation, and another: "Martha, thou art bustled." The Greek suggests that he speaks it gently and with a touch of pity. It's strange he does not invite her and say, "Martha, have a seat," but speaks only a rebuke, which traps her in her lonely role: "Mary gets it and you, my dear, are a lost cause."

But then a gap. In the style of all the Gospel writers, Luke is terse and leaves loose ends. I know, though, that Martha turns beet red and blusters back to the kitchen, and Mary, with quiet apology, hoists herself with great effort from the feet of the Lord and follows after her sister.

"Why did he have to say that?" Martha says. "And, Mary, these *dishes*." The pile is enormous, the guests so many.

Mary nods, tucks behind Martha's ear a piece of hair that has startled loose from her severe braid.

They eventually do the dishes. "He didn't have to say it with such *pity*," Martha mutters, steel wool to the pot. The dishes take a long time. They get into their nightdresses exhausted. Mary studies the sky through the window, reads from her book of scientific wonders, aches sideways toward her sister, wanting to help. Martha pretends to sleep. Martha aches for a new story.

And the next day, to my astonishment—and you might not have expected this either—it is Martha, out of her square heart, who calls the number on the billboard pasted with five-foot faces of foster children. She chooses a love target and goes for it, willful and bullheaded as ever, but I appreciate her ingenuity, her attempt that will put her on a path, because I need to know this is possible—the heart-melt, the river-shift, the life-again. Maybe you do, too. A story forms inside the husk of the other.

ON THE DAY THE CHILD COMES, Mary makes a snow drift. (It makes sense to begin with Mary, for whom love comes easily.) Well, not really a snow drift. Leaping goat-like and fat, Mary wears no overcoat, only a thin dress, so we can soon see it's not snow upon the bank of earth, but a pile of feathers. In their manyness they are snow, they are whipping cream on cake, they are the in-nards of a beautiful duvet, all for the child. Mary adds a fistful more that she found beside the killing cones outside the henhouse and from beneath the wind turbine and in the radiator grill of a semi. Leap and squat: she peers close-up at plumed vane fastened to rachis—that shaft like a sail's mast—each vane, closer up, com-prising a thousand barbs, feathers within the feather, each with its own tiny shaft and tiny sprouting barbs. And at the bottom is the dizzying downy afterfeather, loose fuzz meant for birdwarmth not flight, a fine poof out from which pokes the hollow calamus, the quill, that once met birdbone or birdskin. *Afterfeather*, Mary says for the sound, having just finished the bird anatomy chapter in her book of scientific wonders. Flecks of red, she will explain, are cardinal, or possibly tanager. There is the blue jay's, the vulture's, the plain swallow's, the dove's, though most are from the hens, a sawdusty white. Somewhere in the center—like a marble for the girl to find—Mary has buried one blue feather from an indigo bunting. She tried to show it to Martha, but Martha was a vortex of Pine-Sol and Clorox readying the house.

Mary will have the girl hold this blue feather up to the sun and will say, Do you know this blue is not the blue you think it is? The bunting feather is gray in dull light, is not blue with pigment at all, but its blue comes from a structure of scales that reflect a blue wavelength of sunlight into the eyes. Mary moons over it, this gift to the gaze, this blue blaze. She reaches her fleshy arms around to keep the feathers fluttering a bit, as though fluffing a pillow.

Of course, it's Martha fluffing the actual pillows and making the bed with hospital corners. The foster child will stay in Lazarus's old room since he has pitched a permanent tent among the sheep and vagabonds and only visits now and then. She will teach the child to care for her teeth. Oh, Martha, all sinew and stick arms, having made a study of tactical movements between kitchen counter and stove. And nervous—my goodness, she's nervous—but it's true it was Martha who called the toll-free number on the billboard. The billboard said, above the huge faces of the children, Be a Hero in the Story, which struck Martha's mind like a two-by-four. The woman on the other end of the line said parents are locked up and strung out, we have too many to handle. There is a young girl of twelve, her name is Maud. Could you take her? And Mary, overhearing, brimmed over and placed her hands at her own open face like two palm leaves, and Martha said, Yes, of course, and Mary did a little topply dance and mouthed, *I'm proud of you*, while Martha pinched the receiver between ear and shoulder and wrote down the details.

And now young Maud will arrive this afternoon, and Martha practices her instructions in a way that endears her to me: Here is your bed, here is a corner of wool turned down, here is a dresser with little knobs on the drawers, here is your window open to the sound of the night bugs. Here is your bed, here is a corner of wool…

Here is Maud in the sisters' doorway: a thin, wide-eyed thing, hair red and like a Brillo pad with a few loose coils gone straight. She appears in a too-big boxy dress that would not be so boxy if she were not so stricken. Her collarbones jump in alarm from her skin. The caseworker carries a paper grocery bag of Maud's things, both bag and girl looking rescued from a fire. At the door, Mary, rotund and dressed in her finest, bows as deeply as she is able and produces a chrysanthemum and an agate and a single swallow feather and cannot speak.

"Are you hungry, you must be hungry," says Martha. The case-worker says, "Go on now," and Maud takes slow, tentative steps toward the kitchen following Martha, who has already turned and marched off as though fleeing or running late. Mary produces an-other feather for the caseworker and says, "I think a bushtit, but it's hard to tell this tiny."

IN THE GALLERY OF RELIGIOUS ART FROM THE 1600s, 1700s, 1800s, the painters tell the story of Christ in the house of Mary and Mar-tha, and, though the clothing changes—the era and degree of pou-finess of their dresses—it's always the same dramatization meant to edify by contrasts. Vermeer is all color, of course, his Jesus in a rich navy robe gestures toward Mary in her spot at his feet, her chin on her fist in soft shadow, but his face is exasperated, turned up toward Martha who is pale and in brighter lighting that removes the secret self, Martha saying *But*—. But she holds the beautiful bread, she stands, she is ever standing. Tintoretto's Martha directly chastises Mary in her huge froth of dress on the floor, Martha's eyes glaring downward, Jesus at the table spilling forth his gentle words of life, with disregard for the dishes and, seemingly, for the spat. Overbeck paints Martha with one hand on her hip, pointing to Mary like a tattletale, *But*—, Jesus wagging his finger to admonish. Allori's Mary is more schoolgirl with a moony crush than contem-plative, and his rosy-robed Jesus gestures again to Martha, with her full tray of empty glasses and flask—*Why do you keep missing it?*

Always Martha is run off her feet, playing the martyr. She frit-ters away her time on the worldly and the mundane, no deep-er glow to her face. This didactic depiction goes all the way up through time, to a nineties cartoonish cover of an Evangelical Bible study workbook: Martha all schoolmarmy, Mary beatific, a sort of hippie possessed of a smoky intimacy with God. *Don't Be a Martha* is the title of an eight-week study for the harried single mothers and women in shoulder-padded suits trying to de-stress. *Don't Be a Clod—Be All Heart, Be All Open Mouth.* Forget about what's on the stove and in the appointment book and on the spreadsheets. The women gather in metal folding chairs in church basements with the workbooks in their laps, the back of their minds ticking with kids' lunches, PowerPoint slides due tomorrow, and who will organize the potluck? Resentful, nodding, resentful. The Mary-and-Martha duality somehow just shores up their Martha-ness, not what they'd been hoping for.

Of course, I have taken notes in such studies, balancing the workbook on my lap. Of course I am familiar with that resentment and know my way around a spreadsheet, of course I see myself in the controlling, controlled Martha, the first lines on the skin of my forty-year-old face etching my forehead in consternation. Of course I worry that's why he left, which is why I'm doing this, old sweater pulled close, lantern lit—asking: what if this is not the story you think it is?

What would I paint, given the chance? The thing more secret, there in the crevice within Martha's self—the surprising intimation, the melting, the breaking-forth. Why retread, and limn in gold and fuchsia, the already known?

For Maud's welcome, Martha has made banana bread with lemon and walnuts. She already has a slice on each of three plates and the butter has been set out to soften. She stands at attention, while Maud and Mary sit at the table. Mary rocks from side to side, her thoughts like drifting dust motes in the bright rays of Maud, a girl untethered and flockless. Martha, worked up to invisible stiff peaks, does not move. Maud eats two slices.

That night, Martha spends a great deal of time on flossing, its importance and proper technique, and Mary says at the bathroom door, "I have a surprise for the morning." When they are all in their nightclothes, Martha says, as rehearsed, "Here is your bed, here is a corner of wool turned down, here is your window open—" But her voice catches. Mary notices. Oh, Martha, this will take time. Martha clears her throat. The three of them look out to the air, fresh and black and full.

"Here is your window open to the stars," Martha finishes.

"To the stars," whispers Mary.

THE NEXT MORNING, MARTHA'S FACE flushes over sausage and egg preparations, and beside the sink Mary says, "Won't you come and see?" But Martha says, "Be quick, so the food is hot, she needs her food hot." So Mary slips out with Maud alone, leads her by the hand to the surprise-heap of feathers out back on the bank. Only a little snowmelt—that is, the wind has scattered a few but not many—and Maud spreads her hand into a palm leaf and runs it through the pile, up and out. Mary helps her seek the blue one, the indigo bunting tailfeather, and when the girl holds it to the sun Mary tells her about the blue wavelength, memorized from the book of scientific wonders. Cross ribs on the scales diffract the light to iridescence such that you see something immanent in light that you did not see before. You see reality differently, in all its possibility. "And it's how the birds speak," says Mary, "in the language of iridescence." She takes the feather and slides it behind Maud's ear, like a pencil, and it's easily held in place by her great nest of red hair. "Listen to the language," says Mary. She fluffs the rest, the feathers float up and drift. She shows Maud, close-up, the fine poof at the base of one, at the hollow calamus.

"Afterfeather," Mary says.

"Afterfeather," says Maud.

A FEW TIMES IN THAT first week, Maud takes Martha's hand, but the tall, stern woman is uncomfortable with that and makes for the kitchen, Mary looking on, knowing her sister must find her own way within her own skeletal structure and unfatty flesh. In the meantime,

Mary tells the girl unproductive stories with no arc, teaches her to pray ineffectual prayers, to draw nonfigurative doodles. And Martha tells the girl how it is, from here to there, how to hem her slip—*find* her slip in the first place—unlike Mary, whose stout legs are always visible through her sheer skirt that catches in the bicycle chain.

One night, Maud takes sick. Martha smears Vicks VapoRub on the croupy chest then stands sentinel while Mary comes bedside with her doodles. She draws with black pen, some pastels and pencils. "No need for discernable faces," Mary says to the girl, and she never finishes since they are not finishable, only starts a new one on a scrap, a fury of orange colored pencil and green. Maud wheezes her admiration at this fourth one held before her. "Looks like—" but she can't settle on a comparison, and Mary shrugs, says, "Just *is*." Martha heads for the door, says, "Remember to sleep, I'll fetch the vaporizer, did you floss?"

The next night Maud sits up in bed and Mary sits splayed on the floor making blessing books. "It's soon spring so I want to write blessings," Mary says. She has written them out, Xeroxed them, cut them to size, and now she staples the center to make mini booklets. "See? I have doodled a little something in the corner of each. When you're better, Snuffle-pup, you can come with me to throw these from the car window to the side of the road among the yellow coltsfoot blooms, and we'll get Martha to come."

Maud looks doubtful.

"She'll come," says Mary, "she will."

AS IF MY MIND WERE STILL GROWING, the poet Gerard Manley Hopkins once wrote in his journal and I once copied into mine. It is the way the perfectionist, the workhorse, tries to change: to will herself toward growth. Raised up in the pew, hearing Martha's story, did I not always think, as she toiled, *how unfair*? Think: *she is so alone*. Think: *when the breeze blows, it does not move a hair on her head*. When the day forms, she already has it in her grasp, like a woman seizing a chicken by the neck for slaughter. She does not know thirst or the quenching of it, deep in her body's recesses. Even as a young girl, did I not blink worryingly at the specter of Martha, how familiar her movements were to me, her way?

And does not another failure at love give me cause tonight for data assessment, analysis of the spreadsheet such that the old failures feel potent, only a few columns away? The most recent lover's leaving only conjures, like some hologram, the once-husband, the once-love-of-my-life, standing in our doorway—years ago now but tonight all the same—saying to me, "You have an old hatred in you." His blue eyes startling, my bleary eyes bloodshot, my whole self exacting, in control, unbroken-into, my lists and accomplishments a bulwark around my *missing it*. This was his rebuke, his *Thou art bustled*, and was there not a trace of pity in his voice? An old hatred for what, I don't know—for myself, I guess, my error and ineptitude, my own failure and vulnerability, his. No doubt he regrets saying such a thing—it is a cruel thing to say to someone—but wasn't there a kernel of truth in it? That we can be heir to a kind of hateful shutting-out of the world; that, for some of us, love and lark do not come easily. When he left, it was the only story I believed for a while: you cannot sustain love, you cannot possibly raise a child. I unlearned it, eventually, yes, that it was not my entirety, but our well-trod stories, our too-familiar roles, can come back and haunt us here in the blacker air. In the fresh wake of someone else leaving, how could the old story not catch me again in its grip? But what I am trying to believe is that, within the tired, narrow husk of the old story, it is possible for the heart to shift. Though it cannot be *willed*, it is possible, in time, for a thing strange and new to emerge.

THEY TELL MAUD TOGETHER ABOUT HER PERIOD WHEN IT COMES. Mary with a gift of silk scarf and a kingfisher feather. And Martha with gravity and a voice of decorum and dust, grave but also comprehensive anatomically. Despite Mary's study of science, in this matter, she says: "There's the pull of the moon, and waves, a swish in there, our little pear, how the green blushes pink." Maud receives the tampons and pads and scarf and feather into her lap. "These threads in you unspooling," says Mary.

MONTHS BECOME YEARS, THE YEARS pass, it snows real snow. Maud says nothing, ever, of mother or father or hearth or native land. The sisters keep her; the caseworker simply falls out of touch. Martha thinks often of that first night before the open window, looks upon the three of them in nightclothes with young Maud in the middle, as if from the ceiling, and how unyoked they were and are, how mysterious the child remains to her, how mysterious the mechanisms of intimacy. Yet, it occurs to her one afternoon—it occurs to her quite suddenly as she applies a toothbrush to the stained caulking around the bathroom sink fixtures, and she drops the toothbrush and raises up to see her angular face and her hair pulled back in the mirror with one strand falling free, a thin ringlet—*There are a thousand arrows that have pierced me.* Her eyes water and sting. She does not name herself a mother exactly, even a foster mother. She thinks, I am unnamed the way Mary's ridiculous doodles are unlike anything.

When Maud is nineteen, she gets her heart broken for the first time. She calls out for Mary through the house hallways, wants Mary to enfold her, but Mary is out. Martha is all there is. Maud falls into bed, unable to get up. Well, what to do? Unlike Mary, Martha believes in effectual prayer, and she thinks: prayer like a body folding around you. Martha, so clearly *edged* and skin with nothing to spare, to Maud's great surprise pulls back the corner of wool and lies down with Maud, at her back. Martha folds her body, like an awkward stiff reed smelling of bread dough and parsley, around the bereft girl. Martha becomes all eaves, all shelter. Maud is surprised out of her tears, not least of all because Martha has never lain fetal in daylight, not once. "This is a way to pray," says Martha, matter of fact. "Think of the results, how if you have hypothermia and we spoon skin to skin I can keep your blood hot enough to flow through your heart—also, if there's a grenade and I fold my body around it and take the force to blow apart my innards, I could save you. It's practical, really." Then she stops talking and holds Maud unspeaking.

THE NEXT NIGHT: "You need to wash your hair, Maud," says Martha, "there are caterpillars in it."

"Mary put them there," Maud says, barely audible, Maud the nineteen-year-old with her loud broken heart drowning out her voice.

Martha tramps to Mary's room for explanation, says the caterpillars are strange and red-brown with yellow patches. "And they're *hairy*, what are you thinking?"

"I'm thinking she's sad," says Mary, "and I think her hair will be safest for their pupal stage so she will eventually get to see what they become."

Martha is exasperated—"And what will she *see* exactly?"

And Mary, too, is exasperated, in her gentle way, because it's the blue morpho butterfly she's trying to hatch. "A blue *morpho*, imagine, one of the biggest in the world, it's in my book—eight inches of blue wingspan that is not blue the way you think it is, but structured scales diffract the light so that it's simply the bluest blaze, like some feathers have. I want her to see."

"This will not help her," says Martha, her eyes tired, her voice unconvincing.

"I want her to see and to hear the language of iridescence."

"Will it help?" asks Martha.

"I want *you* to see," whispers Mary.

"I see," whispers Martha.

"Oh," whispers Maud with the caterpillars in residence.

———

THE NEXT NIGHT: "I once survived a hurricane," Mary says to Maud's door because of the heartbroken girl's self-imposed internment, the secreted-away pupae notwithstanding. Mary says, "Our brother once survived being resurrected. I once survived being thrown by a horse. Also a famine. I ate beetles." Maud says nothing. "You will survive this kiss and the kiss's goneness."

Palm leaf hands to her own fleshy face, Mary closes her eyes and says, "You are in the left place, he is gone, but the left, unchosen place is cool in feel and moisture. I can see your thoughts gathering after his odd beauty like dry leaves in a passing car's wind. But where you are, outside love for a time, how shadowed is that place in the cool, where the lamb might lie in the heat of day."

Maud cracks the door. Then, after a moment, opens it wider, her face a reddened wreck.

"But here," Maud says, "is where the arrow went. See? And here the kiss. And the aftersmoke."

"Oh, Snuffle-pup and Bandit." Mary strokes the girl's hair, sort of, it's more like patting a box hedge. "Oh, stranger, native to nowhere," Mary closes her eyes again. "I have to pat you gently to know you blind. I have to learn you. There is so much to you."

Martha shows up, her hair unusually tousled, to make a trio of standers in the doorway, in a clutch. Martha also with eyes closed, all their eyes closed. Martha puts her hand out too, to pat Maud blind, to feel unbelievably close to the girl's roughed-up heart. Because none of them have ended up where they meant to end up, have they? Hands move from wrist to collarbone to forehead to mouth, love moves from need to need to need. From yes to broken-open yes.

"Afterkiss," says Maud.

"Afterarrow," says Mary.

"Afterall," says Martha.

———

I DON'T KNOW EXACTLY HOW THE STORY ENDS the following morning, except that—extinguishing my lantern, going back outside in the almost-dawn—I hug the old yellow sweater to myself but then peel it off, down to tank top and cool air, and I feel the breeze move across Martha's face. It is early. Maud prepares to leave, to go out on her own with her stowaway caterpillars, her pristine teeth, her hemmed slip and favorite doodles, but she and Mary cannot find Martha. It's Mary who's left to fuss over the luggage and the sandwiches, Martha nowhere to be found. Until Maud thinks to look out back, on the bank of earth where there was that first pile. Maud is not sure why she does not look in the cellar, in the pantry, at the wash line, but she doesn't. Mary follows. And there they find Martha, stooped like a bent willow and lightly rising as she gathers a fresh heap. Oh, mostly from the sawdusty henhouse beds, mostly white, such that you might think snow except this is summer and Martha's dress is thin, and these are feathers and the feathers are for the girl who has come, and the feathers are for you and for me. Martha reaches to the center of the pile and unbends and unwinds herself and turns her face so softly toward Maud, for from the center of the pile she has pulled the rare indigo bunting tailfeather. It is so blue unto all the light's possibility, a thing magnificent offered for nothing.

BLESSING FOR THE INCONSOLABLE

MAY YOU REMEMBER YOUR SUFFERING the way hair remembers its braid after a long night wet upon the pillow, a night with windows open and pollen dusting down and also moths, the hair having been plaited after a swim in the river when the tributaries had been high from spring rains and the sediment rich, such that, in the morning, when another comes bedside with a brush, there is only a faint smell of river and the dry, soft waves of hair. Which is to say, may sorrow be softened by enough forgetfulness. Hold the brushed-out leaf bits and driftwood bark in your hands in this wide room, unto the fireplace clean and large, having yielded to the bats threading in and out of its chimney, and unto the little dresser simple and the floor bare. If no succor, then sound, song-bird. Red-winged black in the tremored marsh. If no solace, then slip your hair hung forward to fall down your back in waves as you lift your face.

II.

WE SLIP SLUICEWARD

WHEN I DREAM US INTO
THE BOOK OF RUTH

So she lay at his feet until the morning, but arose before one could recognize another. And he said, "Let it not be known that the woman came to the threshing floor." And he said, "Bring the garment you are wearing and hold it out." So she held it, and he measured out six measures of barley and put it on her. Then she went into the city.

—Ruth 3:14-15, English Standard Version

…she has drawn out of him, with gentle force, a possibility of larger life.

—Avivah Gottlieb Zornberg, *The Murmuring Deep*

I DREAM THE MOVEMENT OF LIGHT ACROSS HER BELLY FREE OF DRESS. I dream her prized cache of castoff things. I dream her bowing down into the goodness of down, where the murmur of her is a kind openness. I dream her first, though, further back—Ruth the Moabite as a young girl in a summer game of kick the can, sensing in the night (I think she could) all that would come. Sensing, even then, the ways we would all misunderstand abundance.

In the unfolding game at dark, all the child bodies hide except the one body looking. The hum of looking falls everywhere in high grasses, eyes tracing each bulge by a tree or shed wall so to call out a name of the seen for capture. The Maxwell House can, empty

of coffee and empty of nails and bolts and tobacco juice, is over-
turned to hood the grubs in the middle of the yard. All are waiting
for one of the hiding bodies, one who is not-yet-seen-or-named,
to come running and kick the can, like a metal bell, yelling *olly olly
oxen free*, setting loose the captives.

Ruth is so good at hiding in the barn shadows, untouched by
the moon spilling in between slats. She is frozen among the residual straw bales broken up by mouse and coon, her hair forward
over her face. She does not want to be captured, for that will make
her known; nor does she want to be freed, for that will send her
down the road unto the forces that will carve her out, like a bowl
that will hold many things.

I want to know her in this pause, as she solidifies a self. I want
to take time believing her and believing in her as she holds her
breath before the plunge into her life, before her time comes to
choose the harder thing. I think she must have, at one time, resist-
ed capture in a childhood game such as this. She holds her breath,
she raises her gaze. Sees a tiny bit of bone from a skull of mouse in
the crevice and pockets it.

The coffee can clangs and flies, someone sounds the call, and
Ruth readies. She slips out of the barn shadow and into her story.

HER STORY IS THIS: THERE is a drought in the land of the chosen Hebrew people, and the man Elimelech travels with his wife
Naomi and their two sons to the fields of Moab, a foreign land. He
dies, the sons seek wives among the foreigners. A young Ruth marries one of the hungry sons of the now-widow Naomi. Ruth dresses and undresses by the fire; she dresses and undresses her young
husband by the fire, with small hands shaking. Ruth is so filled
up, she cannot sleep beside his body because of the overwhelm,
because of the wonder of his breathing, and *This*, we think, *this
beginning promises abundance.* Another Moabite woman, Orpah,
marries Naomi's other son.

Both sons die.

There is a swell of widow heat: a persistent heat, like that of a
desert sandstone at night still radiating old sun into the belly of the
lizard, of the snake, of the small bear where the fur does not coat.
The women are hot in mourning. Ruth can find no cooling creek
but finds the dry bed of a once-creek and gathers driftwood in the
front bunch of her dress, a few sticks tumored out beautifully with
parasite. And, from a distance, Naomi and Orpah watch her: they
see her as a drawing, the twigs like chaotic ticks of charcoal. Ruth
is out there gathering up a decision. She returns to the tent with
her sticks. The three of them stand in the hot wind. Naomi says
to them both, There is nothing for you, go back to your people,
maybe you will make a life. Orpah kisses her mother-in-law's face
and agrees, she flees for a future. Ruth is filled with a great stillness.
She looks to the left toward Orpah's wake where the dust drifts in
the air, she looks to the right where Naomi's just-kissed face is a
used-up washrag. Ruth sets down her driftwood in an altar-like
stack, says, I am already making a life, and she clings to Naomi,
like odor to a corpse, like a fool, and she sloughs the known for the
unknown. She accepts, with this choice, the hopeless, bitter-root
end of widows.

Out of Moab, they return to Naomi's Hebrew homeland where
the Moabite is the despised Other, the cursed stranger. It is a new
kind of lonely in the unpainted tent. The famine is over and there's
a harvest, but the widows are hungry. In the morning, Ruth rises
from her floor mat and washes her face, which is now less young
but still young, and goes out from their nothing-tent to glean on
the periphery of the barley fields, to gather the leftover stalks to
bake into loaves that will keep them from starving. A stray dog follows her three paces back, and she drops him a crust she brought
and whispers a kindness. On her way out to the fields: if she sees a
feather, she plucks it up, if a medicine bottle with a narrow graceful
neck, if any left-behind thing from the duff and moss—a little GI

Joe plastic figurine taking aim—she gathers it into her dress. She studies the small bottle and loves it and uncakes the mud from it. She begins to believe in generosity and, in response to that belief, the earth yields up its gifts.

ONE STEP, TWO, TOWARD A LIFE EMPTIED OF RECOGNIZABLE PROM-ISE. Here a river stone with flecks of mica, here a watch face with no band which she will string for Naomi as a pendant.

Arriving at the barley fields, in the stooping for the leftover grain in full head, she is as far from triumph as one might run.

Except she is carved out, like a bowl, to hold all the gathered things.

Except she is so full of desire, holding it all bundled in her dress with the sheaves and stalks and bottles and berries and rogue apples.

Except she lays bold claim yet is ungrasping as a field lily.

Except she is the fire lit, ready. Can we see by way of her, can we dress and undress, keep warm before her?

IT IS THE FIELD OF BOAZ WHERE SHE GLEANS AT THE EDGES. From the granary, Boaz spies her distant stooping form. The leftover barley stalks she carries look to him like charcoal scribbles against the pale blue paper of her bunched dress. He asks someone about her, he fumbles with his hands, his hair has gone gray, and also his skin, he is not young. He asks, Who is the gleaner there? And hears of her extraordinary kindness to the widow Naomi. At lunch, when the laborers congregate, he bashfully gives Ruth parched corn of which, after she has had her fill, there are leftovers, and he whispers to one of his men, Leave out some of the good sheaves for her to gather.

Naomi learns of his interest. Ruth, she says, perfume your skin, put on a nice dress, go tonight to where he beds on the threshing floor, he is your chance. And Ruth goes, she follows the ridge down, as if the idea were hers, collecting along the way a little chestnut-oak acorn with its too-big cap, a pair of worthless stones, a strip of tinsel. Where he sleeps on his side with knees drawn up, she lies down, as the harlots do on harvest nights, and uncovers his feet and sleeps there next to him (she remembers something, that uncovering, that undressing of lobe and limb before the fire, the bowl of her body holding memory). At midnight he wakes, this hem of coat lifted so his legflesh shivers. He raises his face which is lined where burlap has been pressed, a burlap sack for a pillow, a grizzle of hair, a gray mouth open—Who are you?

I am Ruth, she says in the darkness, and there were things I did not think were possible again. She says, You will spread your robe over me, your wing. She declares it so. A bold, quiet declaration. His hands fiddle with his burlap pillow. Sleep here, he says. Their first night, with the smell of grain and her lavender scent. They sleep till dawn.

She rises before one can recognize another. In the dawn's dark she is a stranger. Neither is he recognizable, she has made him a stranger, too, wondrous to himself. She has awakened mystery in him, and it unfurls in his chest, it is a kind of enlargement. He thinks but does not say, Come press your hand to my head, your lips to my ear. What he says is, Bring the garment you are wearing and hold it out. She does and he fills it and they part as gauzy, marvelous strangers. He loves in the way a man older rather than younger loves, which is to say he bundles up six measures of barley into the front of her dress. And she? She loves the way a widow loves, which is to say, her emptiness is only a readiness. Which is to say, in time, she will place his shy hands on her belly free of dress.

THIS IS ONE SUMMER OF EVENTS—Ruth heading, driven as a mare, down the ridge, dressed and perfumed, to the granary floor. Peer into an evening of the life they will live together: the small windows all open, she is fully herself and awake, not knowing this was possible, taking him in with an active creation of space inside her, as if setting an inner table. A fluttering of tablecloth with camelias printed on it, a cloth napkin folded in the shape of a rose around a small fruit still on its stem. No window screens, the wind a rush, an exhale of sky into space and somehow space drawing in sky, soup and bread offered on her table and taken, given and taken and drunk, the soup drunk with both his hands around the bowl. The fire is lit, they lie on the floor on blankets. O see all of me, she says—the blond hairs on lower back, then the fact of belly, his swell and rise and taste. The firelight makes the room twice as big when reflected in the large picture window, and they see their used-up faces: *There we are—the leftover, there the ample feast.*

RUTH THE GLEANER PREFIGURES THE GATHERERS OF CASTOFF THINGS, the edged-out people, the widowed, the divorced, the single parents, the orphaned and exiled. A people at the margins of promise. And for the rest of the life that Ruth and Boaz will live together, when he is out walking, he will collect for her the snake-skin and papery penny from the penny tree, the great magnolia seed studded with red-orange berries, lion's mane mushroom furring the tree white, another tiny GI Joe and tailfeather and the medicine bottles of varied sizes, foraged from the field and woods for her.

What she chose was the harder thing: she chose to walk in the lowly place of dust and doom and to see the world as gener-ous and thus made it so. This kind, open light—coming from her belly and chest, her inner solid substance—she shone it with no tie to reward. She took Naomi's bony hand and walked and gathered until she came to know abundance differently in the meager stalk.

Boaz stands there on the granary floor, after she has risen and gone that first time, looking out at a field at dawn when features of the face blur and the being inside each being shapeshifts and glimmers and becomes. His face becomes beautiful. The unchosen Moabite awakens firelit home in the midst of the chosen people.

———

WHEN I DREAM US INTO THE BOOK OF RUTH, you and me in our new love, I see us following after her, trying to imitate her movements, like children making gestures larger than their small bodies are capable of. I try a movement down the ridge: she as widow guides me into love again at midlife.

She lights the fire in our fireplace. She wears her favorite green sweater. In all noticeable ways, she stands in the same place at evening that she stood in the morning. Yet she is changed, having imperceptibly gathered in the good, examined it, each part, as if choosing gemstones or the best meats for a stew, though the things gathered are of little worth. The foraged and forgotten things.

Here: the bafflement and awe, the shaking hands, the awl and the pierce.

She says, I'll light the lamp for you. The wick, the tinder, the fireplace hearth. See your way by me. See how strange the used-up, see how wondrous. They do not know how beautiful they are. They cannot get a handle on it. Or on how abundance is not in the lined larder, it's in the teaspoon of honey, or milk, or salt.

She says, Stretch out your garment to receive.

I see us clearly by her light. All the ways she will open us. And she? She remains, simply trying to gather it all in, like sun-dried laundry from the line, like the dregs, the silts, the sediments, the lees in the barrel. The hints in shadow, away from the dazzling light so swollen with promise.

I FIND MYSELF SAYING TO YOU: We have this now, this feather found, this thrift store dress, this football left behind in my shed. The first cold night of fall, our bodies held, cupping, cupped. Taut flesh where flesh is, in a few places of our middle-aged bodies, still taut, going rigid with cold or pleasure or both, all the windows open.

———

I SEE US THUS: A football toss in the backyard, a divorced man and his son, and the man's heart flares with the underhand spiral, and the son's heart, too, small as a hen's, it seems, only because his breastbone is about that big, in his tiny body in plaid shirt. A charcoal scribble streaks the boy's face, for he started to build a fire in the firepit and he touched the cold coals bearing witness to an old, gladdening flame, and the man thinks, *How will I be able to do this, care for these children*, even while he is doing it. An underhand toss, gentle, to his daughter next, her heart a thrum of heat. The man must receive grace the way he receives a ball found in the shed left behind by the previous tenant. And the woman watches, divorced from another marriage and another life and coming alongside him in this game of catch. She touches the sloughed rattler skin she found, dried and rasping and recalling the snake body now somewhere rediscovering itself. She places the old skin on the bookshelf beside the river rock and papery penny from the penny tree, each of these things an *after*, a gentle sign left behind that whispers: *Now you are beginning to understand that you are already making a life.*

The children sleep. The woman lets the man talk and loosen one button, two, of her dress that was bunched full of bruised Ida Red apples in the afternoon, the apples now dropped to the sink, the dress stained a little with apple-rust, the smell of pie and open-fire kettle-dark butter all held in hope within the blush of the scavenged Ida Reds—that cellar-and-sun smell unsealed with a bite. It is this dress in which she gathered, baring her legs and feet, it is this one he removes. On the floor before the fire which is lit such that it gives the room a space twice as big, the flames and bodies reflected in the picture window. *There we are—the leftover, there the ample feast.*

RUTH AND BOAZ ON THE THRESHING FLOOR THAT FIRST NIGHT: When they sleep till dawn—what is the nature of their sleep? In the great risk of intimacy, perhaps he whispers, You are so kind, or,

You are magnificent as a mare. There are still mornings when she will go to him in the fertile hours, when one does not recognize another, when they are strange and lovely strangers, to take him into her.

Ruth bears a son, Obed, who becomes ancestor to Jesse, to King David, to the Messiah, thus to all possibility and fullness of time and rain and dew and all gingerly laid hopes. Thus, we could read her into a narrative of triumph. We could read her abundance that way, but that might be a misreading. Her green sweater sleeves pushed up, her eyes seeking always in the duff a glint of glass or a feather shaft, some tiny good.

What is the nature of her dream that night on the threshing floor? Maybe Ruth does not dream of her noteworthy descendants, or of a full pantry, or of many-roomed tents of bright colors and gifts. Maybe she dreams us into becoming, you and me. She dreams us gathering and holding each scrap of fabric, each loosed tufted seed, each piece of one another we find and recover. She dreams that we may apprehend, in hints and murmurs, the bounty that will never tally.

MERCY'S SMALL ENGINE

revs in the distance. A chainsaw she hears one hillside over, somebody starting the workday. She fills an empty Cool Whip tub with
water for the stray dog who has shown up at her door, fusses with
the burrs and takes tick inventory while he gulps. She kneels eye-
level with the mutt and wipes pus from his eyes with her hair, not
even thinking. Somebody must be sawing up the worrying limbs
storm-blown into the road. In the saw's hum, she holds her hair
and remembers. Kneeling in his pant, his paw thorned but scritch-
ing her knee a little, her children, origami birds, not yet unfolding
from bed.

She remembers that morning taking in the laundry, she who
always loved work and work as salvific. She loved a hotbed in
spring to bend her back over, one part chicken manure to four
parts soil, tomato seeds saved on bits of paper towel and planted, towel and all. The cistern and the smell of apples, keepers in
the cellar beside potatoes growing eyes. The pick-and-wash-the-
peas when the sarvice snow fell harmlessly. And that morning,
she loved the laundry on the roof. Gathered in the wash hung
overnight, a host of cleaning rags, each rag a specter in the dawn.
Unclasped each pin—hands catching the sundried, moondried
like open mouths.

From the roof, with her basket, she saw a man walking, a body
marked for dead. A warm morning, his arms bare and holding

nothing. Marked for dead how? He cast more than one shadow, as if taking on the shadows of others. She was industrious, she had saved money, she was not reckless, but was suddenly desperate and headlong without knowing why. In a fluster, she found the alabaster jar under the kitchen sink and slid into the whole sleeve of the task, her work coming into its full form in that moment. She left her home and hurried down the road with the jar and a fistful of the line-dried rags to the house he had entered. There the man sat, a dark jade to his eyes, coiled large hair, his skin too early creviced with sun and pain and tenderness. She had never met him but knew him.

The jar had no stopper, so she broke it open with a stone, and when she broke the jar it was as if she broke herself. Her heart split under a ball-peen hammer into two halves of walnut pungent with meat. His shoes must have been left at the door of the house. She knelt to where the ghostly spider webbing of sandal still delineated where dust and sun had touched and where they had not. She poured the oil over his feet, a rich spikenard, underground rhizomes of the Himalayan pink bell flower crushed to priceless oil. She forgot the rags at her side and did not see but felt the beautiful bone under vein in the foot as she wiped the oil with her long hair. What a waste, the others whispered, her oil could have been sold to feed people and clothe them. But all she saw was the bathed foot wet like the face of bloodroot after rain. The skin made new like a child's, the skin made ready to die.

GRIEF SHAPES US INTO HUMANS FROM WHATEVER DUST WE WERE. That night she grieved him, cried until a croup cough took hold and she went out into the cold night air to pry open her lungs. She wanted the shock of breath. Outside, the peepers in the reservoir were so loud, rending sky from sky with song. Sometime in the middle of the night, when the chorus frogs died down and the sky was one, she slept.

Come morning, she pulled on a dress and her sounder shoes in case of snakes. She would let the nettles have her legs. She carried cold ham and fresh peas out of the city, taking careful joy in her limbs that insisted: joy, too, a shaping force. Once she crested the hill out of the weeds, she ran along the fencerow where there were new lambs and the fierce sheepdogs warned her away but she ran closer and closer to the lambs slick and startled. She quit running where the fence gave way to thicket and ditchweed, her heart in her throat, and she did not have to be told the news of how he died, her love now emptied out of jar and limb and vessel. She could not describe her breathing body then except as an empty hull flooded with feathers.

No one knew her name. When the wind blew west she was a whore, when it blew east she was an acolyte, when it stilled and hung heavy she was simply someone at the start of her workday. The Gospel writers piece her together, the woman with the alabaster jar anointing the Christ and his Passion. There in Bethany, or maybe it was Galilee, on a steep slope of the Mount of Olives, near Capernaum. Maybe in a black goat-hair tent, or in the mudbrick house with window shutters opened to let a stripe of light glisten the oil into excess radiance. The scholars have spent centuries trying to say who, where, why, what message exactly, what meaning. Hers is a story that never happened but is always happening, and whoever she was, I know she would have line-dried her rags. Whoever she was, I know she would have run the fencerow at the lambing despite the warnings.

She took the clutch of rags with her that day, but, in the end, she used her cloth-rag hair instead, and does so now, wiping the gunk from the dog's bloodshot eyes. The hum and rev of new mercy nearby, someone adding to a woodpile. The children lift limb and limb from sleep and will soon emerge. There is work to do today. Whoever she is, she hears the sweet low whine from the dog long roaming through fields of dew. She buries her hand in the matted fur over his heart.

A THOUSAND FACES

HARD TO BRUSH THE WEST TEXAS WIND FROM MY HAIR. All the silt and mesquite smoke knotted up. One morning he climbs the hill, always with pen and notebook, whistling like a surreptitious bird to let me know where he is. The mist rises from the river warmer than the cold air and, still in camp, I pull on all my thermal layers and start to brush my hair. Same long johns and wool socks, same enormous Chihuahuan Desert silence, his man-size self gone small up on the bluff. I spend considerable time on the knots, then climb the hill to him, following turkey and wild mule tracks across the washes, passing signs of an old firepit and possible shelter, some cans and glass—no plastics, so an old site. Despite the leave-no-trace protocols, I always want to see the traces, am heartened by somebody's edibles wrapper, the old blue glass, a shoe sewn together many times then discarded at the camp on the Mexican side where they once made wax from candelilla. From the hilltop, we can see across the few miles to the canyon we've just paddled through. Downriver, a ranch, an old water tower, the invisible sound of someone starting an engine.

WE DROVE OUT HERE TO WEST TEXAS FROM VIRGINIA, canoe strapped to his Subaru roof, to paddle the Rio Grande through Boquillas Canyon, to see the world laid bare. Seeking the most elemental sort of revelation: stone unto wind and water and all stages of winter light. Revelation from the Latin stem *revelare*: to unveil, uncover, lay bare. We wanted to see how a three-million-year-old river has unveiled faces in the canyon wall, cutting the rock downward over time as the western rim of the Sierra Del Carmen rose. How the slow river has shown the path through limestone and shale slope to the feral horse and the lion.

We have made this trip during the Covid-19 pandemic. We minimize contact at gas stations, keep rubbing alcohol in the car and masks on the dash, aware the Texas infection rates are dismal. We both teach at a Virginia university on winter break, the job still fairly new for me, and our middle-age togetherness, after failed marriages, is fairly new as well, just over a year old. I harbor that basic desire, too, then, to know more deeply the person I am coming to love, to have him laid bare. May we see each other's faces in a new light, out of our semester routines. From motels on the drive out, he calls his children nightly at their mother's. I still have no children of my own, and that I also carry, a question that might yield, who knows, under desert light.

It is late December. We have shifted our noses to the southwest, like the lucky beasts we are.

IN MY HAIR, THE WIND through the carrizo cane, the black phoebes crying out, tying knots.

COME, MORNING, AND REMAKE US and all the grasses and silver-iced trees and the rye grasses, the butternut trees. A small fable of revelation from my childhood: A girl heads out, in the late-fall cold of hardwood mountains, to make a leaf rubbing. How to choose— the poplar, the black walnut or sassafras? Dawn pinks up her face; she takes her time choosing. She picks up several to press in a book, the serrated and veined, all crisp with color. She holds each petiole, the midrib like a tiny spine.

For the rubbing, she chooses a sugar maple glowing gold-orange-red as if painted. She sets the leaf on a smooth, hard place and overlays her paper and rubs her charcoal flat-side down. The outline says hello. Into being comes the jagged lobe, the gutter of sinus, a lobe again, and another, the bones clean in their bright-dark presence. She loves how the leaf is remade on the page torn from her notebook, a full nothing until the charcoal scrubs and discovers. This is revelation.

In this fable, the girl is growing up in a tucked-away mountain church and thus learns young about the tablet of stone with God's law written by a finger of fire. So, the next day, the girl likewise puts a torn sheet of paper to a granite slab carved with words—no leaf, only the stone itself etched with commandments. She lays the charcoal flat-side down and rubs, and there appears not script but a face. There comes clear, in the rubbing of the ancient words, a distinctive face. Like magic. She wonders at the trick. She reaches back for something she remembers: when the first holy face came into focus over her near-exploding newborn heart, she batted it with the tiniest heel of hand, with fingers like caterpillars. The hair fell forward and framed the large face of mother. *Show me*, was her infant cry. *Reveal to me who you are.*

HE AND I ARE HERE TO PADDLE BOQUILLAS CANYON where the river is slow and shallow enough, in winter, to walk across between Mexico and Texas. We've planned carefully for the thirty-some-mile stretch along the border, but one must hold plans loosely. In the motel on the drive out, I read *Desert Notes: Reflections in the Eye of a Raven*, an early book by Barry Lopez who died a few days before, on Christmas. *You must come with no intentions of discovery*, he wrote as a young man about the desert. *You must overhear things, as though you'd come into a small and desolate town and paused by an open window.* Sure enough, a sudden snowstorm blows in, a cold front swift and decisive, and dumps a historic foot of snow on West Texas. We are marooned, with our intentions, in the small town of Sanderson in the motel off Highway 90, a two-and-a-half-hour drive from Big Bend National Park where we planned to put on the river.

There's nothing to do but wait out the storm, canoe atop the car like a ghost of itself, the cacti around the motel shrouded in drifts off the highway. The Stripes truck stop across the road buzzes with jacked-up nervous truckers, and we hear Interstate 10 is impassable with no snow plow for a hundred miles. The last time this happened, we learn, was in 1986. We settle into Room 12 at the motel, Outback Oasis, next to the snakes the motel owner Roy catches to sell, though it's been a bad year for it—too little rain, five inches total for the year, until this storm. Roy is also scheduled to be our shuttle driver. In a room off the motel office, there's a Mojave rattler behind glass, a Trans-Pecos copperhead, a tarantula, and secretive scorpions.

Faces washed cold, hair unwashed. In bed he reads me a surrealist poet. It's almost a new year. Almost 2021. He writes bundled up on the porch on a wooden bench made in Mexico, I at the makeshift dining area by the microwave and mini fridge and the blasting heater. We write essays and poems, knowing no other way to be in the world. We make love and watch the bowl games and repack our gear: one spoon, one blue enamel cup, two pairs of long underwear, a propane stove, an idea of trying to pray, though I have forgotten my prayer book. There are always things we forget. I've brought notes, though, on the passage in the Book of Exodus about Moses's desire for revelation; as is my habit, I've packed this biblical story to sense its currents in the new story unfolding. Also some carrots and peanut butter and a taxonomy of desert plants.

We're hopeful the road through the Chisos Mountains will soon be passable. We wait out the storm with trucker coffee and tamales, microwaved ham and cheese sandwiches, New Year's Eve champagne he brought. He learns there are caves beneath the Sanderson water tower and heads out before the snow is too deep to look for the rumored arrowheads for his son. Before the snow really started, we climbed the hill above town to look at the small football field built for a six-man team, the Sanderson High School Eagles. The only green in the whole town was within the radius of the field's sprinklers.

Now blind prickly pear and lechuguilla in snow drift. Cholla and yucca encased in ice. The snow on the Chisos is legendary; it's all over the news. He refills my trucker coffee. "We're basically locals by this point," he says. Go Eagles.

The day before the cold front moved in, it was eighty degrees and we went walking on Indian Head Trail near Terlingua to see the petroglyphs, faint traces on red rock. None of the drawings on the rocks a clear face but still a kind of face revealed, a some-one making record. "It seems like something about birth," he said, touching the faded outline. Then he realized he forgot the firepan, and we had to drive an hour and a half north to find one in the larger town of Alpine, Texas, then back to Sanderson. We drove under the spectacular sunset sky, careful of road runners and the huge elk standing on the shoulder, careful of the darting coyote.

HARD TO SAY HOW LITTLE WE KNOW, but I believe it's less than we thought. So restless, we wash our faces in cold water again, emerge somehow younger, all the lines and folds of our skin notwithstand-ing. It is late December, and then it is a new year that begins with drifted-in agave and spares us our expectations so that we might receive the gentle astonishment that has come. It's like something precious wrapped secretively in a ratty cloth, as if to say: You don't know what you came here for, what you want laid bare. The snow-melt will green the desert weeds—in middle age you are lush (you don't even know how lush you are). You are no droughted des-ert—the droughted desert is no droughted desert. Stay soft as the impossible snow.

———————

FROM THE STRIPES, I SPLURGE for our New Year's dinner, micro-wavable fried chicken and a Butterfinger and a decent Texas IPA. I keep my nose to the wind waiting for the warmth from the south, pull on his oversize boots when he is back with his could-be arrowheads, break new track in the drifts along Highway 90.

COME, BONEMEAL AND LIME, PRAYS Moses for the meager crops, this prophet intimate with morning. In his story of revelation in Exodus, he comes up from the valley. *And something to deter the cabbage worm, and something for the calf scours—cider vinegar in the milk.* Rising from his tent before light, he tips out toward the makeshift barn to look to the cut in the mountain through which the sun will first spill and bathe his face. How seen he feels, how never shadowed, only sheltered. Dawn light caressing, it changes and rearranges his pores and lines and age. He closes his eyes to the wash of first light, then feeds the goats. He knows the secret of morning, what it means to bring the flesh of his heart, as if a blank tablet of stone, for the day to be written on.

BEDRAGGLED MOSES IS TRYING TO LEAD THE STIFF-NECKED PEOPLE OF ISRAEL, slaves no more except to themselves and to their insatiable wanting. They have just gone through the ordeal of the golden idol—they threw all their bracelets and rings and spoons into the pot over the fire to melt them into the shape of the calf that yesterday had scours. So desperate, after their exodus from Egypt, for a visible god. So sick of the rumble of thunder and floating fire unknowable in a land hard and wild, where each clump of spiky grass disabuses them of pride. Angry over the idol, Moses broke in two the first tablet of commandments at the base of the mountain.

And Moses is a man also weak with wanting. He will plead for God's presence to stay with them; he will try again to get for them the law of life, the law that beats in each strong and volatile heart. But first, he climbs the rock face seeking something for himself. "Yield, stone, yield," he mutters. He too wants a visible God. From up there, into the brutal day, he says: "Please show me your glory."

God says, "I will pass before you. But you cannot see my face. You cannot see my face and live. This my jawline, this my lip." God tells him to stay in the cleft of the cliffs, to slip into the cave where bears and bats seek refuge. Like a small nest carved into the mountain above the river, from which a man might see and hear the osprey and the screech owl. And God says, big with life, "I'll cover you up with my hand as I pass by, then you will see my back."

God says, "The nape of my neck, but not my face."

"Okay," says Moses.

As God passes, man and bear and bat brace when a wind that might burn skin and fur blows by, the cave mouth covered, then— a shape of a great back that has borne and will bear all the not-yet and the now and the always. Then—a still air, a falling wetness like a heavy dew coating thickly, like when manna rained from heaven and the quail gently fluttered the gifts of themselves down to the desert floor to be meat for these people. The nape of God's neck laid bare. Not touchable, but there, evident and evidence of something, even if only the notion of connecting skull to spine, if God should have a skeletal structure, that place where a low braid starts on a girl, where you cup a person to pull them in for a kiss.

Come, nape and skin expanse, folds of skin of back and body— who are you? Moses, startled, weeps for what he sees, his own skin now emitting light such that he can see the stalactite and guano and webby cactus bones left over from the bear's meal on the cave floor.

After two days, the storm breaks. The desert sun is huge and relentless again, melting the world. The cholla is learning a new lap in its winter survival: ice that has rarified each hair-spine now soaks in. A foot of snowmelt like a gust of greening—the Chihuahuan Desert will come into hues other than rosy sandstone and brown scrub, even if it knows it can't get used to it. He checks the CFS levels, the river rising just a bit so the canoe might not drag as much. Snow on the tops of the Chisos like something dreamed. We crumble the rest of our road bread for the Mexican jays and head for the river.

FIRST DAY, WE PADDLE ABOUT SEVEN MILES INTO CAMP, canoe heavy with gear and nine gallons of water but buoyant in the shallow river. There's still snow in the Sierra del Carmen to the south. We pass hikers who wave until we enter the mouth where Boquillas Canyon is reachable only by boat and then we pass no one. At one bend, only a canyon wren singing. At another, a bell clanging lightly on a donkey's neck as it moseys through the bamboo-like cane along the bank, eating willows. In the creosote bush that smells strong in the shade, flash of white—a feral horse, Mexican side, US side. Hard to tell, all day long, the swallow nests from the pores in the rock face.

At first camp we pull the canoe deep onto the cobble bar and set up near the mouth of the side canyon, then gather firewood, rock hound, take photos, catch the last light scribbling in our notebooks on the riverbank. High sixties today, then the evening desert cold falls quickly, but the limestone walls hold sun, and we have our thermal layers and mesquite to burn in the firepan. The cool air presents no threat and I feel grateful we waited out the storm in the confines of a heated motel room.

We choose chana masala from the backcountry pouches he ordered online—we choose from Louisiana beans and rice, biscuits and gravy, scrambled eggs. Add hot water, stir, and seal. Looking up from the driftwood fire, I say, "There's Cassiopeia, the W," though I'm not sure, like I am of Orion's Belt. I think I can make out the oxherd boy waiting for the wild magpies to form a bridge across the Milky Way to his love, the weaver girl.

He loves the great swath of stars but doesn't care much for the constellations, the stories in the sky, maybe because they're a way to keep from seeing the sky, the star shooting at your periphery. But I love to see the faces and horse bodies and great bears that others have seen. That first night, my sleeping pad springs a leak and the cold ground creeps into me, and I am all sharp hip bones. We can't find the leak so we have to share his pad, as close as two people can possibly sleep, so many miles from any others like us.

IN THE MORNING, INSTANT COFFEE, then we hike up the side canyon that keeps going and going. We find a foal nursing on a feral mare. "It's like swimming without having to go underwater," he says, the rocks like coral reef, fossils of shells embedded in stone. I find a piece of shapely mesquite and seek another for him. The driftwood has faces, or looks like bone, the old bark like flayed skin. Dead, it has life-light in it.

If you'd take a rubbing of the limestone boulders here, shells would appear, you'd reveal signs of the sea. Everyplace there are signs of Long Time, the river carving through stone. Limestone holds the story of rose quartz and ocean, the smooth river rocks I pocket and driftwood-with-light-in-it all bearing witness to the surrender of things to water and time and the large quiet air. And to the rare snow—remember—and to the sun that finally makes it down to the canyon bed in late morning. It's time for oatmeal with dates, walnuts, dried cranberries. Then pack up and shove off in the canoe again.

THE TRUTH IS, I WEPT when we came into this first campsite as I hoisted up from the gunwales and stepped onto the silt mud and stones. We the lucky beasts in the canyons and the washes and the cobble bars. I wept for the beauty of it and for him sharing it with me, having been here before ("Just wait," he'd said, smiling, around each bend as the stunning canyon swallowed us deeper in). The overwhelm of it. How much glory can we really stand? Moses said, Show me, and God said, I'll show you what you can stand. See the nape of my neck, my great body after I've passed, the way you see someone leaving a room and taking his story with him and you know you will long for him.

He said as we came into camp, "I saw a thousand faces in the cliffs today." Up on the limestone walls, his squinting eye seeking something south-facing. A nose, a brow, a chin. We do see faces in the rock face. We do see the known in the unknown. We cannot help it. The canyon wren, though, we do not see, we only hear it, and only once.

AFTER GOD PASSES BY THE CAVE MOUTH, revealing a broad back, God's voice coaxes Moses from the cleft: "Cut yourself two tablets of stone, like the ones you broke in anger, tables clean and scrubbed and carvable, and I will write the words again with my finger. Be ready by the morning, and come up alone in the morning to Mount Sinai."

Moses, jittery, takes the stones to the top of the mountain alone, even the goats and sheep and cattle tiny specks far off. He knows the secret, what it means to bring a blank tablet, as if it's the flesh of his own heart that is ready—as he deflects his gaze away to the ground and sky—for fingerlight.

God hidden now in a pillar of cloud. Each letter etched with fire into quicklime flume and ushered out. The law shows up by means of some linguistic presence in stone itself, as if God can find word in stone just as God can find water in stone, light in darkness, food in the dearth—all that quail and bread in the scrub from out of nowhere. Moses wonders whether such words are written or, instead, revealed as if, from the first morning, they were always waiting to be found. Either way, it's a full nothing and then—

Moses closes his eyes and runs hand over stone like the blind. He feels the word of our heartbeat: *Thou shalt not kill.* He feels something like a figurative contour in it: one being recognizing another being as holy. One commandment among the ten. And Moses feels his face glow again, as it did in the cave, his skin fired in a kiln. A great change comes over him, the way dawn always changes him, but these changes now are denser. He labors down through the crags to the people and livestock and tents and worries below. The people are afraid when he descends with the tablets; he draws them to his fierce radiant skin. He finally puts a veil over his face, for he sees the harsh shine of it in their eyes and on their hair.

He has brought down the fire-chiseled law from on high. He cannot sleep in his tent that night, face itchy, body feeling at once like balloon and boulder. He still sees God's back passing, like a stampede of horses but all flank and tail and hind limb—not the wild rearing head—like a horrible storm that is over but has left on the skin a burnt ice. Like a child disappearing before you are able to call it beautiful. He has put the tablets away from himself, in a tent all their own.

Why, he wonders, can no one see God's face and live? Why only your back from the cave mouth amidst the awful winds? Is it because we cannot handle the magnificence and loveliness, as though we can bear to see only rough surfaces and approximations because the real thing is too much a burden to live with? Too much revelation for us to hold and still stay intact and function? Or is it something else? Is your face something scarred or deformed?

What does it mean for you to hide your face while you etch with fingerlight the Law of Life—*Thou shalt not kill*—which holds in it the command: Look full in the face of the other, mar not that face. Strike it not from the world. Look to the other's face and live.

WE MAKE GOOD MILES OUR SECOND DAY, paddling flat water basically, so little current in the sluggish river, and we feel the effort in our bodies. The morning moon stays with us, slowly sinks into the cliffs close to evening. The second night we camp at Rabbit Ears, a clear formation aptly named, towering over the water on the Texas side. Lots of donkeys today, horses, bulls roaming, a bull bluster-ing out of the cane to glare at us from a weedy island. Distant bell as we drag ashore the canoe, a snort from a donkey far up on the bluff, wanting nothing to do with us. Evidence of beaver work on the water. It's a warmer night, with a southern wind. The river gently noisy, the willow branches scratching the tent fly in the light breeze into the night. Still, when darkness falls, I dress in all my layers before I pee in the higher grass, gather driftwood to burn, pull out a few small pieces to keep, one beautiful bleached piece for him. Beans and rice tonight, firepan light such that all we see is one another's face. Star light such that all we see is everything. "There's Cassiopeia," I say, unsure again of the lopsided W, our little joke now.

In the middle of the night, the burro sounds his desperate bray right outside our tent. We startle and laugh and I worry he might eat or stomp all our stuff, straw hat and salami. I curl into the inner curve of his body sleeping fetal and the wind picks up, the willows talking. Even with the shared mat, he rests out here like a boy.

In the morning we explore the smooth box canyon as far as we can go before we're barred by a wedged fallen boulder.

"Was that donkey a dream?" I ask.

"Definitely not," he says.

I tend to the camp and fill water bottles from our multi-gallon jug. He sounds his bird call until I find him, a speck with a note-book and binoculars, up on the bluff where there's rainbow cactus and lots of inner webbing of prickly pear like old beehive or tiny woven wire. Through his binoculars, he watches a pair of peregrine falcons move in and out of the canyon crags like mates. I wonder if he looks at me enlarged. I stretch out on the grass chomped down to its roots by the roaming beasts and watch the same falcon pair in their distant smallness and grace.

The folds in the rock look almost tender, like spooning lovers. I lie looking up at only sky, sun, raptor, rock and think about Teju Cole's book *Human Archipelago* that he wrote with the photographer Fazal Sheikh, responding in short lyrical sections to Sheikh's photos of faces, of backs wrapped in scarves, of boots left behind. A book of strangers and Cole asks who, really, is stranger and who is kin? Writes: *We are folded beings. Our skin, which is our interface (the word is carefully chosen) with the world, is a zone of folds.* We are not so different from rocks in our foldedness, showing the pressure of time, except that we are a blink of light and they a long open blaze of millennia. Our inner and outer folds bearing witness to time and to story. Loving another seems to mean wanting to see these folds up close, to be folded into them.

COME, MORNING, AND REMAKE SKIN and hair and thoughts in your light. Reveal the day: brewed coffee, eggs, and whatever the kids think up. On a given morning back home in Virginia last fall, I turn to him in the last of his sleep, his bearded face, eyes shut to seal in dreams, little crusts there. His lips puff out breath, the vein at the temple pronounced like when a headache starts. I rub his temple. Today, he and I will both teach our college classes. His kids will give their book reports. We will all mask our faces. We will all wonder, in our own ways, whether the world is lonelier or less lonely as it moves from place to place in face coverings, as we all keep distant because of risk of infection. The world is certainly less touched. I have never felt the luckiness in touching another's bared face as keenly as I feel it now.

But is there not a new kind of tenderness as we pass each other with cloth stretched over nose and mouth, noting the wet and crinkled eyes and the brows arched in worry or surprise? I do miss the mouths of others, the beautiful teeth that structure the face, the jawline and nostrils flaring like a horse's. But there the graying hair at the temples, there the receding hairline and creased forehead. I miss the face but in some ways am more moved by its hiddenness.

"What you see above, in the eyes," he says, "it's expressive." He is a good teacher. The first day of fall classes, he was so glad to be with his students, young first-years giddy to be out of their parents' homes even though they are allowed only so many in their dorm lounges, must stay at six feet away and not touch. Even though their Rwandan classmate must join online when the sun is setting for her and it is morning here. They watch the morning sunset together. They are together.

Togetherness and revelation look different now.

I HAVE BEEN THINKING OF EMMANUEL LEVINAS'S PHILOSOPHY OF THE FACE, rereading his interviews in *Is It Righteous to Be?* The face is the word of God, the seat of ethical relation. *It is not a metaphor,* he says. The face *is the way in which the word of God reverberates.*

What does the face say when I approach it? This face, exposed to my gaze, is disarmed...all its weakness pierces through and at the same time its mortality, to such an extent that I may wish to liquidate it completely. Why not? This face of the other, without recourse, without security, exposed to my gaze...is also the one that orders, 'Thou shalt not kill'... The face is the site of the word of God, a word not thematized.

I pull these ideas into the context of the mysterious Exodus story and the story of now: Moses was told no one can see God's face and live (*you may see my back*), yet we must see one another's faces *to* live and to keep from killing. And, yet again, we must, at this specific moment in history, hide our faces to keep each other alive.

I've often wondered what Levinas meant. I've loved the poetry of the face as central to our salvation, but what does it really mean in lived life and relation between me, my lover, my lover's children, my students, my parents, the child I may or may not ever have, the child I may seek to adopt, the stranger before me, the stranger I have never met and whose face I cannot see?

I get closer to understanding Levinas reading Judith Butler's *Precarious Life*, written during the rise of war after 9/11. She quotes his essay "Peace and Proximity": *The face as the extreme precariousness of the other. Peace as awakeness to the precariousness of the other.* Attending to a face means being awake to the other's vulnerability to suffering. And *face*, for Levinas, does not only mean the visage itself. He speaks often of Vasily Grossman's *Life and Fate*, a World War II novel, and Butler quotes a passage from the book:

Families, wives, and parents of political detainees traveling to the Lubyanka in Moscow for the latest news. A line is formed at the counter, a line where one can see only the backs of others. A woman awaits her turn: [She] had never thought that the human back could be so expressive... Persons approaching the counter had a particular way of craning their neck and their back, their raised shoulders with shoulder blades like springs, which seemed to cry, sob, and scream.

Each person in this line, Levinas says, is *reading on the nape of the person in front of him the feelings and hopes of his misery... The face, then, is not the color of the eyes, the shape of the nose, the ruddiness of the cheeks...*

So, the opposite of the face can be its revelation. During the first years of our war in Afghanistan, Butler writes, the newspapers featured the bared faces of Afghan girls now free of their burkas, and we found in their bareness our achievement, with little understanding of the burka and what it might mean in terms of liberation, community, culture, sex—we could see in the girls' faces only our version of freedom, a version of ourselves. *The American viewer was ready,* writes Butler, *to see the face,* to possess it, to use it as a justification for violence. *Where is loss in that face? And where is the suffering over war? Indeed, the photographed face seemed to conceal or displace the face in the Levinasian sense, since we saw and heard*

through that face no vocalization of grief or agony, no sense of the
precariousness of life.

A girl's bared countenance may obscure the humanness of the scarved and storied face unto which we might be more tender than triumphant, into which we might read vulnerability and uniqueness and holiness. We are a stiff-necked people. Think, in our long history, of when we have not been awake to the true face, when in Civil Rights marches Black sanitation workers carried placards in the streets of Memphis: *I Am a Man*; and now a migrant girl holds a placard in a refugee camp on the Greek-Macedonian border: *We are humans like you*; and now US protestors carry placards: *Black Lives Matter* and *Dignity for Asylum Seekers*, seekers crossing this very border traced by this river. We must say out loud truths so holy-hushed and inherent, all because we have grown hard and gone blind.

I come back to Moses's plea in Exodus, Please show me who you are. From the mouth of the cave looking upon God's back in the searing wind, the springs in God's shoulder blades—it is a different kind of revelation that I can't fully understand, except that there is surely intimacy in it. Except that you might read in it all of God's loneliness and love. Were I Moses, crouching in the shelter of a cool limestone cave, I might ask to see God's nape in the first place. A word I love, *the nape of the neck*, where a low braid starts, where a skull ends at its divoted base, where you cup and hold. In the ancient story, maybe there in the nape and shoulder blades is God's deeper expressiveness, the only way to show a people hard and blind. *Here I am, revealing. Come see, you small proud beasts.*

IT'S ON THE THIRD DAY that we see the dead mountain lion.

Maybe we came here to be awake to Long Time so that we might have perspective on our small sorrows and the larger sorrows of the world. To put our hands to the rock wall that gives way and stays softer than our brief fleshy selves can understand, its beauty revealed in what it has yielded, what has been carved from it. Can we say, even, *these tender canyons?*

We paddle mostly flat water again. We scare heron and a hundred sunning turtles, hear more than see the ravens, see a flicker of a tiny green bird we're not sure of, like a hummingbird but not—green jay maybe, or orange-headed warbler because the green is subtle. We see a pack of javelinas riverside bolting for the cane when we come around the bend. The carrizo is still thick but browning here, as we near the end of the canyon. We've read about the invasive cane, about attempts to eradicate it with parasites, controlled burn, poison. Border Patrol knows there are sometimes families hiding there, and maybe we are seen as we pass by. But we neither hear nor see recent signs of others. We hear only the soft clanging bells and see only the hoof tracks of livestock that cross back and forth with no sense of boundary. We do come upon an old raft with paddles, moored with large stones, waiting, maybe, to help someone cross with their belongings. But that's it. The rest is hidden.

I hold the canoe on shore as he scouts a small rapid and finds, on the wide cobble bar, the dead lion and walks me over to see it. I learn later that if you find one, usually it's headless because someone has taken the skull. He does want the skull but there is no taking it. We cannot bring ourselves. The ear cartilage is still intact and pointing up as if the cat were still listening, the paw still looks like a paw, though the guts have been eaten by scavengers. It lies on its side. He does take a tooth, a canine. And claws. I take two claws from its paw, they slip out like pins from a pin cushion. There is a hush and a sadness; there aren't many lions, they are shy and mysterious predators, we have seen only tracks in the mornings. And here, one silent and being laid bare by wind and sun and pestilence and vulture. We can't tell what killed it—did it wash up here? Did it come here on these smooth stones to lie down and die by the peaceful rapid? It is small, probably no more than forty pounds when living and ranging wide in this great expanse. We take photos of the paw that still looks like a paw, of the hide still covering the ribs. This will be a story for him to tell his kids—look at these claws tucked away, think of what these claws once did, once pierced. I love moments like these for him, when he holds memories in the lion's canine, stores them away until he can bring them out at home, set down the tooth in their small palms.

Beside him, I feel more exposed near the carcass under the desert sun, but this is what I asked for, that everything be realer and clearer. In my open palm I hold a layered hush and two claws from the lion still beautiful as its bones begin to bleach under its deteriorating hide. In this place, my questions of love, of children, of how to live, hang suspended in the light above the lion's body. I hear the echo of Lopez: *leave behind your intentions of discovery*. That imperative to simply overhear, catch the warbler in your periphery, see a rustle of cane that could be hand or hoof. Stay lucky, beast.

This third evening, we camp four or five miles upriver from tomorrow's take-out in La Linda, the abandoned mining town. We're out of the canyon now, buttes in the distance, in more open country. And we're wetter today, from the knees down, from lining the canoe through some rapids. The day was warm, but now we're out of our wet things since the cold will come quickly. We settle into the routine of tent, driftwood, inflating the single sleeping pad, choosing, this time, the biscuits and gravy pouches. Two beers each for our last night. A surprising flock of noisy turkeys trails along the ridge in silhouette, and he calls out in a garble and they answer. In my bag with my journal and pen and few books, I stow the two claws tugged loose from the dead lion's paw.

Out here, I can better understand Israel's melting down of gold spoons and bracelets into the shape of a calf idol, seeking the known out in the vast unknown. Yahweh's miraculous Red Sea parting dismissed as dream, the manna and quail a figment, surely, just a trick of the distended belly. But idol is not revelation; it is not real. God must be something harsher and harder to know and soft as limestone, which I now know to be soft, and more intimate with us than we can comprehend.

He and I wake to dew and frost, to an earlier sunrise in this open-sky camp, mist rising off the warm river. He burns a morning fire as he makes our coffee. He climbs to the bluff; I brush some of the knots from my hair. Somewhere, on a ranch, an engine starts up.

We're early to the take-out that afternoon. We wait for Roy, our shuttle, soaking in the last of the silence together. Roy kicks up dust and noise as he pulls up the Subaru and we load in. On the drive back to Sanderson, we see a zone-tailed hawk and patches of unmelted snow, the freak snowfall seeming so distant now. Roy gives us a room at Outback Oasis for the night, and the shower is glorious, though it will take many more to wash the mesquite smoke from my hair.

The room's thermostat is broken, so no heat but our bodies, which is all the heat we need. But we can't sleep. "It's because there's no river sound," he says when we lie awake in the motel's queen bed. We camped in the canyon by the soft rapids each night, the putter of water over rock bed barely a rush-roar.

The next morning: a fresh pair of jeans and a clean sweater for the two-day drive home where he will pick up the kids, we will prep our courses for spring term, we will enter another uncertain year of Long Time with the rest of the fragile world. We leave before dawn. We carry with us the same questions and desires we hauled out here, but they are newly inflected. And we have been shown some things in the winter light on canyon walls.

I HAVE COME TO LOVE THE SMALLEST PARTS OF HUMANS, like the chin to touch, like the ear to kiss and lightly bite, like the uneven brow and heel of hand. All call out, in a morning breeze before the heat, *Do not kill me.* Do otherwise. Kiss me, or wipe the mud from my cheek. Keep me alive until, in time, as I must die, my skin going threadbare, you take a cool washrag and wipe the chalky dust from where the skull is starting to show through.

ANOTHER SMALL FABLE OF REVELATION: Just before fall classes start up, he asks me to swim with him in the lake. I have so many tasks but change into my swimsuit and swim because soon it will be September—the water will be too cool to fling my body into—and because I want to see his face as it comes up out of the water. What a brief and tenuous hold we have as fall descends and dark comes early and years layer like hand over hand over hand. I love how the faces of his children break the surface of lake water like those of seals.

PERHAPS IT'S TRUE THAT TENDERNESS IS THE ONLY THING THAT CAN SAVE US. Perhaps that's Levinasian. The refusal to harden with knowing-already. Staying soft, staying beast that nuzzles beast. Make your leaf rubbings, see the faces that show themselves in the wood and in the folds of skin there and there, all around you, in the throng.

WHEN I DREAMED MY CHILD'S FIRST DAY OF SCHOOL

she was so happy to go, the bus her hot air balloon. Up into the ribbons of sky. So early in the morning, I was silhouette in the doorway to her. I was happy too, to lose her for only the brief day and to have the zipper sound of her pack, the *click* of her lunch box in the cool air at summer's end when you're saying goodbye to so many things, like the rhododendron, which you know will come back. The day got ragged after I woke since the zipper sound was so real but the child only a dream. I touched zippers. Touched and watered the laurel I planted past bloom stage, touched the four-dollar Goodwill shirt I got for my love to wear to work, a Land's End shirt very professional with all its buttons, and I knew that, at the end of the day, I would admire the back of it as he'd lie belly to floor to blow the fire to life in his fireplace, all the windfall sticks gathered for kindling by his children. I'd put my hand to his back, a good wrinkle-resistant shirt. I'd hear the kids talk on the phone in the next room to their mother from his first marriage. I said to myself, Lay out your blouse and pencil skirt for work, get it together. The strange refuge of outfits. I said, Think about finding that shirt for him on the thrift store rack and picturing his chest and arms filling it up like wind or straw, like a foretelling. I made myself remember all the happiness I've known, none of it owed me. I remembered the dog shoulder-shot, flesh hanging in ribbons, coming up the yard of my childhood home and not dying. I remembered squatting to pee at the river's edge under the moon as my love sat by the campfire and watched me gather my dress. I remembered a breeze through the screen and finding my mother's iced heart sugar cookies and new pencils at my child-place at the kitchen table, a memory intact like a plum. I remembered clasping sandstones on the cobble bar and filling my pockets and filling bowls back home and there, too, taped to the wall, a tail feather of a heron. Still, sometimes all you want is the ease of losing something whose body, slight and decked out in new little jeans, will later return home to fill your doorway with talk. For that kind of brief loss, there are days you would give up everything you've been permitted to keep, things with no leaving and no sweet coming-back.

WHEN THE SEASON IS FITTING

for Diane Gilliam

There was a priest named Zechariah... And he had a wife from the daughters of Aaron, and her name was Elizabeth... But they had no child, because Elizabeth was barren, and both were advanced in years... And there appeared to him an angel of the Lord standing on the right side of the altar of incense. And Zechariah was troubled when he saw him, and fear fell upon him. But the angel said to him, "Do not be afraid, Zechariah, for your prayer has been heard, and your wife Elizabeth will bear you a son, and you shall call his name John... and many will rejoice at his birth, for he will be great before the Lord."... In those days Mary arose and went with haste into the hill country, to a town in Judah, and she entered the house of Zechariah and greeted Elizabeth. And when Elizabeth heard the greeting of Mary, the baby leaped in her womb.

—The Gospel of Luke 1:5-7, 11-15, 39-41,
English Standard Version

MY FRIEND DIANE SAYS: WHEN the season is fitting, a book will come, the words will come. She is a poet speaking on a winter day to a group of writers, me among them. She is discussing Robert Bly's book *Leaping Poetry* and James Still's poem "Leap, Minnows, Leap." In Still's poem, minnows are dying in a shrinking pool because the water is held above the dam; they gasp little fish-gasps; by the poem's end, they must leap or die, though of course the leap is not sane. Bly, in his essays, stresses the energy from line to line, stanza to stanza, the excising of crud, the line taut and brimming with buzz; each line, too, must leap or die. When Diane speaks of poems, she speaks of how we live our lives, or how we might do so. She says quietly, "We leap and shed the lives we have made." We move from the known to the unknown. At our scuffed tables, we are all writing to save our lives, and maybe also the lives of others, so we must leap from our dying. It is a beautiful and moving lecture, and I sit there teary, taking notes.

I don't remember, now, whether that phrase, *when the season is fitting*, figured into Diane's actual lecture or in a separate conversation that day about the anxieties of production, writer's block and so forth, but the phrase appears among my lecture notes and doodles of small desperate fish. The phrase suggests inordinate trust and calm, not resignation so much as acceptance, a kind of active waiting, or active reception, a readiness, a preparedness for *this*. It calls for a living-into-time without fearing the ravages of time. I see, in my notebook, how I finished the phrase with trial words pulled from my fretful midlife heart: When the season is fitting, a child will come. How lovely to consider:

A warm rain. On the porch of rough lumber, my fella and I together, screen door leading out to it with a driftwood handle he's made us. Talking until we're too cold. Talking to be held by one another's voices. Evening falling, bodies slipping inside the house. From his mountain of duvet, an arm sneaking out to wrap me. And the baby, like day breaking into me—all this instead of yesterday's pale substitute: my offer to hold an infant, ever sniffing out mothersmell, for the young mother in the checkout line while she rummaged in her purse for her Kroger card.

What if the season is not fitted exactly to our plans?

I return to the idea: leap without knowing. This requires trust, too, of course, leap of faith. This is very hard to do. The concepts are related: trust that what is coming next is the right thing. Leaping is like being born, being born unto time with no expectations of time except opening eyes and ears and arms.

Right at this moment, it is I alone on the screenporch, the scavenged driftwood waiting on the table to be put to use. Though he has mentioned making a door handle, it remains an idea. I confess that I fear the word *barren*. Not that it's a word we use much anymore, not that as a woman and writer and professor I judge my worth by childbearing. But the word is still a word, and it's spiny like desert plants. And I'm reminded of the biblical story of Elizabeth, cousin to the Virgin Mary and mother of John the Baptist, how she was *long barren* but then conceived John in old age. When Mary came to visit, pregnant with her own child, fetal John *leaped for joy* in the womb. Another kind of leaping, little minnow in a water sack jumping while still having tissue and organ knitted together and cells festooned with DNA. On my porch, I love this story, another old story with newness hidden in it, with its dynamic movement from the known to the unknown. I am filled up with Elizabeth, under the porch roof, studying her movements as day breaks.

ELIZABETH—THE RED OF THE RED cardinal fills the gap in the tree. She loves the single note of red through the back door open to the good of January, the bracing breath of dawn. The sky is clear and the sun-on-snow squints her eyes, though she is aged and her face a sheaf of pages on which years of snowlight have written; the squint goes soft. She steps onto the back porch, sticks out her face like a girl looking up the road to make out figures coming. It's true that sometimes she sees the faces of babies.

The porch is raw lumber, the wind is raw wind, the waterfalling creek is mostly ice, the house-heat is gone. Elizabeth's simple face is a prayer ongoing: *Here within me is a way made for you, it is wide, it is lined with yellow wood sorrel and phlox, there is a warm light.*

In the mudroom, she pulls on dress and boots, ties back her hair, washes her face. The stout woodstove in the kitchen that broadcasts heat through the whole house has gone out. She shakes down yesterday's cold ashes and cinders into the ash pan beneath the firebox, dumps them into the bucket in the mudroom and steps out again to the porch where the wind is raw. Hair strands dangle. She stands there in her dress unafraid of the real work given her to do, her desire frank and silvered and relinquished.

Elizabeth hauls the bucket across the snow to the edge of the woods. She dumps cinder and ash on unbroken snow, hearing a whoosh not unlike a blue heron lifting off, leaving a blurred arc on the snow, not unlike the blue-blurred sky. An arc of ash like the stroke of brush on canvas. This is the season of the ashes. She sets down the bucket and, in the shed, fetches an armload of wood, feeling the density of the locust and cherry. *When the season is fitting*, she says, *I feel the rough of the rougher bark.* There is the season of emptying the ashes, the season of tying back hair, of yanking on boot, of the pressed oak leaf, of a walk in high grasses holding palm level to the tips of sedges and rye, the season of the roasted sweet potato with oil and salt. Nothing but this undertaking, like a globe filling her hands and then, in time, another.

Now tinder in the firebox, match to the tinder.

Because the other women in the valley have borne children, she is called barren. But she does not know the word or use it. Before the rain, she is full, after the rain, she is fruit. When there is no rain or snow, she prays, *Take me to the river*, she prays, *Flood and fill me at the river*, she prays, *Wreck my bones onto the riverbanks, you river within me, you river never without me.* She says, *This the blue of the blue sapphire.* She says, *This the stone of the stony cistern. This the snowlight from the unbroken snow and the beautiful arc of ash upon it.*

She is old. It's true she still desires a child which is no longer possible, but she is ready nonetheless, she prepares herself for everything: her living-into-each-task is that readiness, preparedness. I watch her leap, all old skin and sinew, letting that skin shed, slough off, her bones full of light emanating out: *I am here, I am willing.* The mind flayed before the unexpected, a daily leap from all she has known to all she does not know. *I am ready for this, this season fit for rushing in the high grass, for you wind in the grass, you wind never without me.*

A girlface looking up the road, making out figures coming her way.

WHEN YOU ARE READY: IT is a poem you make with your whole body, the body fevered and the body in early spring that goes to a lover's bed like a farm dog to a bed of clover with tiny purple blooms and variegated leaves.

The light spilling and pooling, over clover as over our limbs, our small mountain of us. There is a bit of moss, glowing, almost as if with late frost. We do not know what time will bring us. Today: a polka dot dress, and a night to remove it in one swish.

There are times I see the faces of babies, knobby and mon-keyish, and feel all the heat creased there in new cells smelling of green, maybe of moss, new as a frost is new.

ELIZABETH—HER PRIESTLY HUSBAND ZECHARIAH, TOO, is old. He has gone off to the temple. There she is, coaxing the wood-stove back to radiance, still in her January dress and coat and boots, hair tied, also making slaw with apples and honey and pop-pyseeds, when he returns late morning from burning incense in the temple where he was told in a vision that he and she will have a son. He did not believe it, so the angel struck him mute. He enters the kitchen in this quiet rush, not knocking the snow from his boots, makes signs with his hands she cannot decipher. She touches his face which is cold, his mouth a sweet O of gums and tongue and teeth and bright silence. For some reason she opens all the windows. The cold sweeps in. *Come dark, come morning,* she says, *I'm here.* She gently pulls him to the bed and undresses him—he gestures, points at things—kettle, kindling, rag, thigh—trying to name them. She puts his pointer finger to her lips. She lays him down on his side and fits her body into his chest-belly-leg curve. Out from the duvet, his arm escapes, reaches around, palm pressed to her breastbone. When they make love, it is a sweet season—and how suddenly she who is old feels the rind of melon thicken, the uterine lining flush full, the dark cells swerve across permeability and nest. The little minnow takes his impossible place in her dark.

How I imagine her sometimes, my one-day daughter: The sudden chill of a spring evening catches her suddenly, when she's been long at playing. She is on her blue bike, having sold the butter to the neighbor and pedaled home past the moss beds frosted and wet, the sun so suddenly nowhere. I can sense her small legs growing cold, the thrill it gives her.

My desire to know her is frank and silvered, my body and mind the simplest they've been since girlhood.

At creekside, I am learning from my love the spring ephemerals: he teaches me dogtooth violet, bloodroot and bluets, trillium and trout lily. And where the secret morels emerge in the duff at the base of poplars. There is a trust in the season of spring coming. My body can close around the empty space of her, the way a yellow trout lily blossom closes around the evening cold.

He shows me the small fragile hepatica on the creek bank, its lobed leaf. Its slight stem barely holds up its face, a neck to take care with.

Elizabeth—Each morning, after conceiving, her face sticking out like that of a girl looking up the road, she faces the green that is coming. Thick into the green she goes, from January into summer into September. The road so empty it's full, she can see the figures, a band of tramps or dancers. The bucket of ashes or bucket of scraps for the possums, she is steady from season to season. She grows round, she prays her prayers, she moves, as always, toward the unknown. She pulls on her husband's jeans when hers no longer fit. She lets out her dress waist.

Elizabeth soaks the peas and plants them and strings the fishing wire, stake to stake, to be ready for the vines that will come. When it's warm enough, past threat of frost, she sows the zinnia seeds, the marigold and radish. In a blank book, she presses petals fallen from the magnolia, a clover, too, and a pink spring bloom of which she does not know the name. Within her tremulous imagination, inside the mind of one with a body swollen in miracle, things are so lush and sudden, so free of habit and habitual thought, so bright and present-unto, so much *this* in the center of her palm: a lettuce-seed furriness, like iron shavings dragged by the magnetic pen to make a moustache on the face, or bushy eyebrows in that clever old game Wooly Willy.

Strands of hair fall about her face held so near the cupped seeds. She does not care to wear her hair up, bound, just now.

THE COWBOY COFFEE GRINDS IN MY TEETH LIKE SILT. What if it's true that there is no such thing as barrenness? That the girlface looking up the road, the girl picking up a bucket to go—as girl as woman as old woman—is as full of miracle all her life as when she is harboring a budding boy? Her underarms wet, tongue to pencil or brush. Focus, precision.

I seek it out. The trout lily. I make a little booklet of the spring ephemerals. I scribble the date on the stones from the creek bed he and I traipse in muck boots. I am always coming back, unhelpably, to how to make a prayer—like one makes a paper lantern or a paper football or a bird feeder from Dixie cups. I am always coming back to desire. I seek Elizabeth's help with living alongside desire and, finally, shedding even that.

ELIZABETH—THIS IS A SEASON of shivering new tendons, bone knitted to bone, a sleeve of skin and downy hair. The child blooms there, beneath belly skin papery with age, in its many pieces and parts: a folded leg, small soft-meat of penis, increment of ear, one infinitesimal pinky nail like a slip of something that could catch in her teeth. She prays, same as always: *Here within me is a way made for you, a small pond with a small fish in it to welcome you, some cattails.* When her relative Mary comes to visit, she who also has a miracle child inside her, Elizabeth's boy leaps in the womb like the minnow he is. Elizabeth strokes her protruding belly, she knows that leap: from what you know to what you cannot quite dream is coming. He will be called John, he will be a baptizer, a prophet, dressed in camel's hair and a leather belt, eating locusts and wild honey by the creek she has always loved.

Toward her own belly, Elizabeth says, *O collective braided thing of you—I don't want to know how you work. How horrible-lonely you'll be in your loose belt and concavity showing ribs, or how you'll love the loneliness as though bred for it like a cattle dog keeping distance alongside the warmth and pool of herd, the way so wide in you.*

WHO IS SHE? I FORGOT to ask that question of Elizabeth first. And does she not ask it of me? She does. She asks: *Who are you? What do you seek? In what ways do you prepare your heart?*

JOHN—HE IS BORN WITH THOUGHTS already fat in his head. When she holds him in her arms, he is a little sack of sleep and fire, and his mute father Zechariah sounds out words again with wonder, like someone speaking for the first time. The boy suckles and then, so soon, squirms into flight, running just to run, beating the stick with the stick. He is like her in his heart: *I feel the ocean and sky in the tiny eddy of the creek I poke with sticks, I feel the eternal in the day*. His mother leaves the door open to the porch all day and all night, letting in the bats and bugs, so he can run in and out. This towel with which she dries her hands at the sink he will not let her dry his head with, his willful curls, strings uncut.

WHAT IF WHAT WE THINK IS BARRENNESS is simply a season other than we expected? I love that she loves the red of the red cardinal. One is making a nest here in the camellia outside my window.

Sit here in your dress on a bed unmade, as a self unmade and remade, and let stir a willingness to take the leap. There is some other thing ahead, something coming that you cannot know. There is no hint, even, of what it could possibly be. It is not prefigured by your hopes, but it is just as lush and sudden, like the spring evening chill that catches a body off guard as this body traipses home.

JOHN—ONE EVENING, HE SITS AT the table sullen. The waterfall beside the house in the rainy autumn is fuller than the drought summer has let it be. There is a stopper in his mouth, like a dry sock. He is not allowed to be bolder than the inside space, the inside space is drought—*Use inside voice*, his father Zechariah says, he for whom words always have a lobed largeness to them now. But what can inside voice carry? Hardly anything. His mother knows, but his father tries to manage him. His watery eyes to his mother: she knows he *is* the creek waterfall and the sun and the shine of the lake, with all the other boys looking on.

He can taste the husk of locust and the flake of the flaky honeycomb.

He goes out to the raw lumber porch in the raw wind and caterwauls.

I LOVE THE PART OF THE STORY when the boy caterwauls and breaks her open. But, in truth, when I weep, I weep for the part long before that, before all the miraculous occurrences, for the beautiful part when she rises up an old woman and quietly, on her plain and simple mornings, utters the word *prepare*, prays: *Prepare me for this season which is fitting.* And takes up cinder and ash, streaks the snow which is trackless but for a single set of bird prints. Gets a streak of ash on her cheek. In the snowlight, in the meeting of want and trust.

ELIZABETH—THIS SEASON OF HIS CATERWAUL, his bark, his unafraid front facing everything, his hair never combed. Even now, her age slows her to sit more often and gather her strength and breath. Still, she pulls on muck boots by the creek with her boy— minnow—shoot of green light.

Maybe it's a season that will be always, him yowling like creekwater swollen in the gorge, swollen and brown and foamy.

When asked later how it felt, she will feel the wholeness of life indiscriminately and say, *He came like a package of crackers for the gulls, or a found feather. He came like a prophet to our doorstep in his sleep sack and then left for the teeming crowds to sound out with fervor the word* prepare. Of course he would be the baptizer in the rivers of the wilderness, he would make way for the one whose strap of sandal he saw himself unworthy to untie. Of course the baptized people would break surface coming up and wear the faces of babies.

She will say: *I felt unaccountable joy.* She will say: *I was so ready, unto every season that came, all the picking-up-the-bucket-and-going. I touched each moment as with palm down, brushing the tips of the sedges and rye. So ready, but nothing could have prepared me for this.*

TO LEAP IS TO PREPARE YOUR PEELED AND FLESHY HEART FOR THIS SEASON. And what arrives this season—like a figure coming into visibility and detail on the road—is anybody's guess.

JOHN—O LITTLE MONKEY SELF, you'll make tea from cleaver and

spice bush. You'll chew the birch bark and string your legs into the limbs of the sycamores, hovering your face above the water like a dog about to lap, thinking, *What is the nature of water?* the water with which you will baptize. Over the rounded rocks it can flow with that kind of miracle, drain from each beautiful person's eyes and ears and return to rush and to seep in the ground. *Who are you, water?* that is the question, not *what*, and then—the one will come with spirit and with fire into which the weeping cherry blossoms do not fall and float, and that is beyond your small sphere but point to it up the road, your face facing it, making out the figure coming.

Today, John seeks out trout lily and violet, lit by his hunger-light, and in this way he prepares as he has seen his mother do. Prepare the way of the Lord, straighten the crooked paths, bring the mountains low. Prepare your heart, its fleshy beat and beat, to explode like a star. To hold so much more than is possible for it to hold.

He will tell them: *Ready your hearts at daybreak for what is coming, for what is here now, on the stoop and in the pantry, pull on your boots.* He touches the fragile hepatica on the creek bank, such a thing to take care with.

I AM FILLED ON THE PORCH WITH HER AND HIM, right now, under roof in a cold spring rain. I'm papery as any, fearful as any, filled to my outermost cells and hairs with desire. In midlife, I long for a child I do not have, so my longing pries open Elizabeth's, or hers mine.

Why does she help me, her mind lush and sudden and quick? Not because I expect that my womb, too, will fill, but she helps me trust the fittedness of the season. I can wash my face at the wide sink, tie back my hair, pick up the bucket and go. I think of my friend Diane gently pushing us to leap or die, slough skin so our bones emanate, the white of the white bone vivid and keen for feeling. Leap and shed even the most intricate desires you have made, or at least the great heaviness of them.

When it is fitting, we bed down, we fill the house with sleeping. We lift our faces to the road. We taste meat and fish. We have bread. We have more than bread. We have less. And even less. We sing. We write these words. We find good words with which to say the things we do not know how to say. We do not miss out on the thing that arrives. We study another bygone story to figure out how to be born. We figure out there is no such thing as barrenness and there never was. May we believe this. May the snowlight find our skin. May we rise up with the faces of babies.

ANSWER WHEN YOU'RE CALLED

Because I love to know the names of things: "gneiss" and "schist," he tells me at our campsite. The stones on the Chattooga River. Names not so roundly sonorous for poems, but the stones themselves are smooth as butter, little eggs you could eat. I rock-hound at each cobble bar where we drag our canoe ashore. Soon the zippered pocket of my life jacket is a cheek stuffed with grapes.

It's late May. We're middle-aged lovers who have found each other years after our respective divorces. I still have no children of my own; he shares the custody of his two, who alternate between homes each week. A few nights before we left them with their mother, his daughter asked me in the lamplight, "Will we have to call you Mama if you and Papa get married?" "No," I said, "you have a mama. You can call me by my name." But my answer didn't feel right, and as we drive the five and a half hours southwest to the Chattooga, her query stays with me.

My lover has paddled this river for thirty years. This is my second time accompanying him. We plan to go twenty miles across these five days, camping in three places, along the stretch between Rabun County, Georgia, and Oconee County, South Carolina. Tandem in the red Dagger Caption, with its vintage Royalex body, we wear straw hats. I kneel in front, paddling on the left side, he steers from the right, doing the harder work with the J stroke and the pry, kneeling in back. We move swiftly through the world on our knees.

On the beaches where we make camp, we each find abbeys of soft stone, take our small notebooks to receive strings of words we love the sound of as we try to name a feeling in its particulars, or perhaps not the feeling but the wonder of having felt. We are describers, scribes, rusty and eager in this work after a just-finished semester of teaching. We separate to scribble and then return more whole to tent and fire, trout and beer and sausages. It seems a principle of love to respect each other's abbey, tufted by laurel and elderflower, then come back together. Sometimes at the fire we read aloud what we've tried to name.

I am ready to be a student of the river, to have the river's names in my mouth and on my pages: gneiss and schist, doghobble, catalpa, hellgrammite. And the river's name itself, Chattooga, which is thought to have come from the Cherokee village Tsatugi, a word meaning either *he drank by sips* or *he crossed the river*. There's something more than the names, something previous, that we are both trying to learn, because of course if you go back far enough, the Chattooga wasn't called anything at all as it swelled and splashed over smoother and smoother stones. Just as richly itself then, as a nameless river.

ONCE, *NAMELESS RIVERS FLOWED THROUGH NAMELESS VALLEYS INTO NAMELESS BAYS.* So opens George Stewart's 1945 book *Names on the Land*, an account of America's naming. *Then tribe followed tribe, speaking different languages and thinking different thoughts. According to their ways of speech and thought they gave names, and in their generations laid their bones by the streams and hills they had named.*

Some names would be great, known far and wide: states and metropolises. Many more would be little names known only by the locals: the swamps and gulches, particular riverbends and sluices, the prolific creeks. Names too small for maps, arising from need and proximity. *Wherever men live, there must be a hundred or a thousand little names to every great one.*

Stewart doesn't claim a sure beginning, but in his study of the history of place names, he posits that the first layer has its origins in utility, name as signpost, usefully marking the place where beavers made a dam so you could find that place again, and only later as commemoration: this is the place where a hunter impressively killed a panther. I'm reminded of the naming in biblical myth, cairns stacked along a journey to mark a transformation: Jacob of Genesis wrestled all night with the angel and would not let go even when, at dawn, the angel dislocated his hip, until it blessed him and said, "Your name is no longer Jacob but Israel." Jacob-now-Israel demanded the angel's name, and it said, "Why do you ask?" and refused. The renamed Jacob called the place Peniel, *face of God*: "For I have seen God and lived."

Sometimes places were named for a vision rather than an actual event, a dream dreamed there of killing a great panther. Again I think of Jacob of Genesis, his dream of a ladder with angels ascending and descending. He woke to a place haunted for him now by angels and erected his stone-used-for-a-pillow as a pillar, poured oil on it, and called the place Bethel, *God's House*, though the place was already called Luz, perhaps named for someone else's dream.

A name takes on a life of its own, regardless of origin. The beaver dam may wash away, the signpost now obsolete; people may forget the event or never learn about the dream. Eventually people shrug, not knowing, or they make up new stories to explain, sometimes bungling the original name as it passes down the generations in a game of telephone. Names become a record of remembering and forgetting, dreaming, redreaming, stealing, a record of first scaling a shale slope, then bulldozing the slope to make way for something new. A record of wrestling with someone who will not reveal a name.

REVEAL A NAME AND REVEAL A CORNER OF THE WORLD AS TRAIPSED, as touched. Early on, I came to know the terrain under my feet by who belonged there during my childhood. I suppose this was about land deeds to a degree, but more about contact, plow and hoe, who swam hunted tilled, who tended the beasts grazing in that field, who let you pick their blackberries. There were plenty of absentee owners in the West Virginia mountains, but no one knew their names. Just as a housedress on the wash line evokes the body that wears it, so the roads and pastures of my rural home—Whetsell Settlement—evoke the people who roamed there. How many times has that saved me? Helped me remember what I am: a body walking briefly the thistled, sedgy ground.

In William Goyen's novel *The House of Breath*, there's a passage I reread often: *Who am I, bruised so unreal?—what will realize me?—I whirl round and bobble or stand like a statue thrown into the stickerburrs. . . . Then I name over and over in my memory every beautiful and loved image and idea I have ever had, and praise them over and over, saying, Granny Ganchion, I touch you and name you; Folner, I touch you and name you; Aunty, Malley, Swimma, Christy, I touch you and name you and claim you all. It is like a procession through the rooms of this house, saying, now this is the hall and there is the bottled ship and the seashell . . . and here is the watery mirror in which, behold, is my face. . .*

The narrator's longing and need are familiar to me. He is only able to find himself, "realize" himself, by acknowledging and blessing his origins, even though—or maybe because—he is forever returning home only to leave again.

I took him—my love with whom I've begun to paddle rivers—to my homeplace, where I can bob my hand fencepost to fencepost and say, "I touch you and name you." Name you Chidester name you Whitehair Wilson Felton Jeffers Bell. He and I rode bikes around the Settlement. I could not give him geological formations or landmarks or histories, only say, "That's over on Whitehair," "That's down Gerasimoviches'." "That's where Eric is building a cabin," a quiet boy on my bus whom I desired once. "Down that path is Sislers'," Liz Sisler's chickens loose in the yard, her next two generations nestled around her in houses built within a stone's throw. Kids I went to school with now all raising children, and the pang rose up as I pedaled. The Settlement is a place where every woman is called Mother and I was now a visitor biking past with a man whose children I love and am helping to raise, who don't call me Mama but do call me to play Scattergories and to come see their carved jack-o'-lanterns after dark. The dissonance between my adult life and the culture of my childhood community tinged the homecoming with mourning, as it does for Goyen's narrator, but this is a grief that enhances belovedness. The wind in my face softened as our bikes crested the hill past Syreta May's and Naomi's and Mary Jane's, and I slowed to a stop and told my love their names, pointing in the direction of porches where, even as a misfit, I would still be recognized and in some deep ways known.

"But I don't know any of these people," he said, which of course I was aware of but could not take in. Looking down that gravel drive, an aisle of ironweed and wild rose, to that dark brow of pines furrowed over the house, I saw Mary Jane's face as clear as a name on a map. Didn't he, too?

DIDN'T HE, TOO, ALWAYS WANT TO KNOW? This yellow tuft, that— what it's called. He who has named for me those spring ephemerals of western Virginia, where we live—trout lily, bloodroot, hepatica, the mimosa trees, and the blooming black locusts. He has written books studded with these names. Walking by the lake near his house, he shows me blooms hanging like small sleepy bells: "Pipsissewa." A Cree name, I read later, meaning *it breaks into small pieces*, sug- gesting that it was used to treat bladder stones. Yes, but even though he's a poet, sometimes he likes not knowing. Prefers that the secret be kept, as Jacob stays innocent of the angel's name. Maybe my love senses that the word we assign may be a deflecting surface. Can a name keep you distant as much as it can draw you near?

Recently, the writer J. Drew Lanham gave a reading at the

college where we teach. A poet, memoirist, and wildlife biologist, he spoke about straddling the literary and scientific realms with their different methods and motivations for naming. I asked how he decides on names, as a person drawn to both ways of seeing. He thought for a few beats, then said, "Take the cardinal, for instance." Naming the bird moves you along a pathway toward the bird; each name establishes its own kind of intimacy. There's the Latin binomial, *Cardinalis cardinalis*, but also the common name Northern Cardinal, also the way his grandmother pointed and called it Red Bird, the spirit of the dead returning. Each name, he said, also draws the namers closer to each other, sharing what they see. The distance between grandson and grandmother, between different knowledge systems, is bridged.

Give me the names for things—says Charles Wright's poem "The Writing Life"—*Not what we call them, but what / They call themselves when no one's listening.*

WHEN YOU'RE NOT LISTENING IS WHEN YOU'RE CALLED. I remember we sat six in the cab, I the youngest of four, the red Ford with a wooden bed like something out of a time other than the 1980s. Who on whose lap? My smaller body on top, near the gear shift, my knee jabbed whenever Dad shifted up to third, then fourth. We almost couldn't tell who was who—four kids in one bathtub when very young, in one sandbox when it could still hold us, uncounted evening hours of freezing our hands in the sand caverns we filled with hose water, which came up frigid from gaps in the limestone a hundred feet down. We shivered blissfully in the sandbox till supper, when Mom would call us in by each of our names, but when she did so, we weren't listening. We were absorbed in that hose-water chill and our sculpted sand, long shadows falling over us from the rose of Sharon and the yew. She appeared at the edge of the sandbox, drying her hands on her apron—"You kids better answer when I call."

———

WHEN THEY CALL THE RIVER BY NAME—canoeists who know the Chattooga by a cross-draw into an eddy—they use the little names. Once they're floating down the chute of box elder and sycamore, reading the water, anticipating each rapid, the river becomes its particulars.

Since the Chattooga is protected as a National Wild and Scenic River, a quarter-mile buffer protects the river corridor—no roads, houses, convenience stores. Which also means a long hike in and out, boat and gear. My love and I put in at one of the rare access points close to Highway 28, then quickly leave highway noise behind, settling into the gentler sounds of water and rock. We run simple Class II rapids first, Turn Hole and Big Shoals. At the bow I have full view of the horizon line, where the rapid drops over each rock ledge, but his view is interrupted by my straw hat and braid and bright yellow life jacket, so on each approach he turns our canoe sideways, seeking the line along the tongue that froths with the highest volume and current. Then we straighten and paddle through together. We run Warwoman, then Rock Garden, where tall stone slabs slant over our boat as we shoot through. Then Three Rooster Tails, its Class III whitewater twirling in boils that bounce us down the river's left channel. We pitch our tent there below Rooster Tails on the first two nights, resting up before running the rowdier rapids of the next section.

I get out and walk Second Ledge, let him run the boat and gear over its six-foot waterfall. I wait at the ledge's base, wedging my neoprene boots firmly between boulders so I can safely snap photos. The red Caption is heavy and mounded with drybags and a cooler strapped to the yoke and thwarts, and for a moment I think he'll tip as he launches out over the falls with a hard forward stroke, but the old boat stays buoyant with a generous splash in the pool below. When he ferries over, I kiss his helmeted head before loading in again.

We paddle the Narrows together, even though the wave-train approach feels ominous and we know the two-part rapid is technical, the river churning and funneling to the middle near some undercut rocks. We hit both holes and feel ourselves disappear in whitewater, but we don't swim it, we don't spill, and I weep with awe. We pull over past the undercuts to bail the boat, my heart racing. We camp at Catfish Bottom, then at a pocket beach near Eight Ball. Eye of the Needle, I walk as he punches the heavy canoe through the wave hole. Also Painted Rock, a rapid bisected by a sharp boulder nicked by plenty of boats that couldn't skirt it. I can paddle the gentle Thrifts Ferry, the wave train of Rollercoaster. The final rapid before our take-out is Bull Sluice, a double drop full of potholes and undercuts. Again I walk it, watching him catch the eddy at the top, plan his line, enter the froth. Many more downriver we won't run, though he's run them all before: Jawbone, Shoulderbone, Corkscrew.

I am new to reading the rapids in their intricacies. But I have my own way of naming that helps me remember. We break off sassafras twigs whose flammable oils burn even when wet, light a fire. And I sit and watch the mist hover over the water downstream of the rooster tails' flailing. I name by braiding: braid back your hair to remember this bend in the river where you made love on the rocks. Where heron and doe hunted, where the water snake coiled in the sun. Braid in your abbey of stone to remember the time, at the still pool beside camp, when you took the boat out alone.

Go out alone in early morning, keep the sun at your back, be careful to do nothing that will startle these timid creatures, and see what you will see. My friend Jim recommends to me Emma Bell Miles, who wrote at the turn of the twentieth century and who let the titmice have her hair for nests. My copy of *Our Southern Birds* is printed with the original plates and sketches and blank pages for the reader's own observations. Miles was no ornithologist; she simply stood still enough for wrens to perch on her arm.

She begins: *While the scientific study of birds is beyond most of us, yet an intimate understanding of them and their ways is within reach of everyone, and may enrich life with a new depth of interest. No line of study opens a more fascinating vista to the mind which wants to know, in the best and truest sense, in what kind of world we are living.* Her focus is the quiet, arm-as-perch kind of knowing. And the book is a feast of names: chimney swift and fox sparrow and pine siskin, where they winter and summer, how they talk, what they bed down in. Grouped by season and sectioned by common name, each careful sketch giving the length of the bird in inches. She trails them to their habitat, the tufted titmouse in a hollow limb *soft with crushed dry oak-galls of last year, with sedge-grass down and hair*, hair from barn floors and also Miles's own head. She rakes hair from her brushes and stows it for the bird to find, but one prefers to rest on her ear and pluck from her head—fine with her.

Miles does not give genus and species, only tidbits about the earfolds of owls, the nests of the crested flycatcher lined with old snakeskin, the sociability of the plump junco *quick to benefit by a handful of finely crumbled cornbread thrown onto the bare ground or a doorstep swept clean of snow.* I think of Lanham's cardinal when reading this book, which is part field guide, part journal and sketchbook, part poem that names not only the swamp sparrow but its trill—*lost riverlet*—which you hear before you see the feathered singer floating on *some light pontoon of chance-caught drift*, past the laurel and azalea that shine bright against the silty bank, like the perennials by the shed.

THE PERENNIALS BY THE SHED IDENTIFYING / *Themselves by vibration alone*—C. D. Wright, "ShallCross." Wright is another poet who finds that intimate knowing means more than knowing a name does: it reaches inside of, reaches beyond. *What is that low-flying short-winged bird / Your mother would know / Even if she can't call up its name.*

IF SHE CAN'T CALL UP ITS NAME, she pestles the herb anyway. Burial spices, burial paste. She knows myrrh and calamus, but not the others. Mary Magdalene, I mean, not Wright or Miles; this other figure from the stack of books on naming, another who went out alone to learn what kind of world we live in, how to recognize it and what to call it. Mary Magdalene reaching the tomb of the crucified Jesus before dawn, hastily dressed, mismatched, no matter since she feels everything as a shroud now. It was a kitchen dress a walking dress a dress for swimming now a mourning dress hung over her killable body. Everything—the lamb in passing; the frog in low, longing song—death will fall harshly upon everything as it fell on him. All the world dead. "This"—she thinks, arriving at the predawn tomb—"this is now the awful gospel."

THE GOSPEL OF MARY. I'VE been reading about this seventeen-page manuscript, missing ten of its pages, discovered in 1896 by a German collector in a market in Cairo. It's been dated as a fifth-century Coptic translation of an earlier Greek or Syrian text. Though not discovered with the gospels of Thomas and Philip in the Egyptian desert near Nag Hammadi, its translation circulated at around the same time, and all three expand the story of Mary Magdalene as an apostolic presence. Sometimes grouped with the Gnostic Gospels, these are not canonical books. The great names are the four gospels in the canon—Matthew, Mark, Luke, and John—the little names apocryphal. Scholars disagree wildly on the authenticity of the so-called Apocrypha, but I am helplessly drawn to the little names.

I'm reading Cynthia Bourgeault's dense exploration of Mary and her gospel that is written in dialogues, Jesus speaking, Peter speaking, Mary herself holding forth about how the divine has worked in us *that we might become fully human*. Mary's gospel reveals an inner circle that includes both women and men—a fact, Bourgeault notes, implicit in the canonical gospels also (*the camp women who followed*) but buried by church tradition. I like to consider Mary Magdalene, like Peter, James, and John, called to be an apostle. These three gospels of the Apocrypha also hint that Jesus and Mary Magdalene were lovers, the popular scandal, and maybe they were, and maybe that is not so scandalous really. Two beloveds kissing as the Gospel of Philip renders kissing: *The realized human is fertilized by a kiss / and is born of a kiss / This is why we kiss each other, / giving birth to each other / through the love that is in us.*

In Bourgeault's sifting through all the gospels, great and small, the moment that interests me most is the one at the fresh tomb. Even the canonical gospels note Mary Magdalene by name as the one who appears with her spices at the tomb and becomes the first witness to the resurrection. There and glowing and beating blood in her mourning dress, with her crushed herbs and oils. The moment is best dramatized in the Gospel of John: she's weeping and looks into the tomb to find two angels sitting where Jesus once lay, one at the head and one at the foot. They ask why she weeps, and she says she weeps because she doesn't know where his dead body has been moved. She turns and sees a gardener, says, "Please tell me where you have put the corpse I love, I have herbs, I have tears yet to shed by lantern and sky." But it is not a gardener she's speaking to, no. And perhaps this scene is indeed a meeting of lovers, coming from either side of death, lovers who address each other with the knowing that came before history, before names.

I REREAD THE CHAPTER "OF THE NAMING THAT WAS BEFORE HISTORY," in which George Stewart sketches a myth of people scouting unknown territory along the great slope of a mountain. The scout notes riverbends to describe later, pale trees in a copse, distinctions for good signposts. He is on the mountain the whole time, but the mountain holds everything, so he does not think to describe it when he gives his report.

This story helps me with the question posed by my love's daughter. Perhaps it doesn't matter what they call me. Perhaps she and her brother can think of me in the scout's way—as a slope they climb on, not needing to name or even be aware of the whole. Here—some cheese, some catch, a swim, supper—your dreams folded into little boats and floated downstream.

Following the ways of the little names, they might eventually call that part of the creek running along my shaley slope Where We Lit Out for the Trail, and that small clearing A Game of Hide and Seek till Dark. Maybe that's how I'll come into small names that feel right. This Little Glade Where They Dreamed.

WHERE I DREAM, ONCE AGAIN, MY CHILD'S FIRST DAY OF SCHOOL, though she does not exist, is in a mountain cabin in the Pisgah National Forest of North Carolina. Pisgah means *summit* in Hebrew, the name of the peak of Mount Nebo from which Moses sighted the Promised Land, which he was not allowed to enter. I shake off the dream and write this passage of my essay in Pisgah, the heart of the Blue Ridge Mountains, so called because what else to call this range? Aptly described, Stewart tells us, in the journal pages of Colonel William Byrd during the colonial westward expansion, as *ranges of blue clouds.*

When there's a break in the rain, I run Deerlick Trail to Gooch Gap. These names find their way into the writing. My sweaty self returns with a fistful of lily and aster for the jar on the porch. I shower, I sit again. The wind is distinct through the poplar trees, whose leaves are larger than those on the poplars back home in Virginia. The view is distinct through this window screen that the June bug battles and the firefly silently explores up and down, blinking as I write past dark. Do I think a certain kind of thought in these mountains? Is my thinking different by the sea? I've scribbled at the Aegean, the Mediterranean, the great Pacific, the littler-named bodies of water, Cheat River and Chattooga and—littler still—Salt Lick Creek near my childhood home, flipping rocks to find crayfish and wading to my little-girl waist. It was not thoughts scribbled into my tiny notebook back then so much as a record of *feltness*, mountain-stream cold on my legs, holding me in that steep ravine that saw only a few hours of sunlight a day. My sister and two brothers dispersed into the shadows to hide for Kick the Can and then, later, gathered for a blackberry dessert made with berries we'd picked over on Whitehair. I don't know why this litany of names—*I touch you and name you*—feels so important to recite here and probe and call.

It is deeply human to name and to touch, actions that might be one and the same—so intertwined that, although I am ever picking up a pen to name and name, I take even greater solace in the naming beyond language. It was my mother who taught me how to name by braiding. She named and cherished the night by braiding my wet hair while the rectangle of dark sifted in through the screen door: this night separated into three parts, this one, this one, now this one, and they come together, and in the morning each part of the name will be remembered in waves of hair like river water smoothing stones.

RIVER WATER SMOOTHING STONES IS the sound we sleep to in the lucky five-day span of tent and red boat and blue enamel cup. He paddles shirtless across to another beach to write and gather drift-wood for a fire, sticks tied with gear straps in bundles according to size. We hear the kingfisher's rattle call, like an engine turning over, then watch it dart downriver. We see heron and merganser, witness a spindly mayfly, the last of an old hatch. We skinny-dip in a light current in the afternoon, roast foil-wrapped sweet potatoes in the coals at night. Sharing a beer, I read him lines about word-less names and the softness of stone. He reads me a poem sequence about the hellgrammite larvae, the full moon, the unfragmented thought he is able to complete when near this river. Firelight glows on his graying beard and on his tall body folded small in the camping chair. "It's going to be in tercets," he says.

Our camp at Catfish Bottom gets early sun. "Want to go out for breakfast?" he asks, and off we paddle upriver to seek shade below the nearest rapid, taking our notebooks and propane stove, our oatmeal packs and cream. We drag the boat ashore, so light when empty of gear. Laurel Grotto, he calls this place, a lone laurel bough hanging toward us, blooming from the rock slab in singular beauty. It's a beauty we don't deserve, the light reflected off the water onto the boulder overhang caked with mud-dauber flutes like humble crusty organ pipes here in the rapid's concert hall. All you can do is be a good steward of it. Study the beating of its wings.

I seek this time the glint of mica schist and river glass, then shift my gaze from stone under water to the water itself. My aging face under my straw hat's brim brings my mother shimmering to mind, and I'm then praying for her, if you can pray for someone by just naming her, and I do hope you can. *I touch you and name you* where you walk in the rye grass, bobbing your hand, *this this this*, touching your sorrows, palm to weeds, and my palm to the silty pool, bobbing. The water is her palm to mine, her care for her ailing mother, my care for kids who don't belong to me, her fears, mine, her hopes, mine, all the nameless things so named by touch.

A stark memory, then, of my father calling my mother's name, Jan, from our porch at two a.m. It was summer, he called over the hill to where Jessie Shaffer lived in the house with asphalt siding, my mother talking with her friend into the night and my dad lonely for her. Calling "Jan," not angry, just asking her to please come home.

I've thought of that again, writing now in evening, when I walk out onto my porch in Virginia and think how my love and I are weaving into the tender parts of each other's lives, such that if we were sharing this evening porch right now, as dark falls, I would say, "I believe I'll go in," and we could close the day together, be the day's envelope. If writing is a way to name and cherish those we love, maybe we do it in the foolish hope that it might save them from sorrow. If there is a way to save them, please tell me how. If there is a place where death does not separate us, please tell me where.

"PLEASE TELL ME WHERE YOU HAVE PUT THE CORPSE I LOVE, I have herbs, I have tears yet to shed by lantern and sky." Mary supposes she speaks to the gardener, but he is no gardener. She turns to go, he simply says, "Mary." She turns back toward him, such an infinitely small thing—two syllables—but all her life comes rushing in, Jesus's recognition peeling hers open. She knows him saying her name at suppers and tutorials and while stroking the nosebone of a lamb. She knows herself as manifold. The name her mother used, the name like a vessel she grew into as her bones and hair lengthened and the wine sack of her flesh stretched, the name she spills and spills out of. The deathless one having the deathward's name in his mouth—smooth ovoid schist, a ripe grape. "Rabboni," she says, *Teacher*, hands to his upright body, his warm face, "I touch you and name you." "Go tell them," he says. She runs to tell them, the first witness to being loved like that. She is still running, through curtains and doorways into houses of sorrow, a bell tolling in the dead silence. She tells them, "You are called." She says, "Won't you answer when you're called?"

WHEN YOU'RE CALLED BY THE TITMICE, you say, "Here is my hair, here I am." Emma Bell Miles—not just a sweet woman mooning over birdsong but someone trying to answer the world. And Mary Magdalene—not just a sweet penitent whore mooning over Jesus but a large aquifer under all the hard surfaces.

Here you go. Have my hair for nests, my buttons for playthings, my zipper for a flash of silver if you like shiny things like crows do. Some flower-print sleeve and this old dress yoke torn in strips to tie on the tree as decoration and for wish-making. Here are all my things, you needn't be my child for me to love you, you needn't know my name to call me—only perch at my ear and sing your riverlet. And so we come to a place of namelessness, you see.

I AM MAKING A PAPER CHAIN, each link moving toward that namelessness. I who love the names of things, who love the scribing, who rise from the desk when my love's son calls, "Come see," to show me the turtle on the trail, when his daughter needs a witness to her cartwheel and wants me to try one myself. There's a letting-go: I am a body following her small self in a goofball twirl in the grass.

I picture a people first loving the lobed luscious names they discover; then inventing, naming anew, out of need; then not quite mouthing names but simply sounding out each round breath that doesn't—they realize—belong to them anymore—fine with them. Thomas Merton wrote: *Love is my name.* Wrote: *Teach me to go to this country beyond words and beyond names. Teach me to pray on this side of the frontier, here where these woods are.*

THE WOODS ALONG THE RIVER DISAPPEAR into a veil of mist the morning we wake to paddle the final stretch and make the drive back to pick up the kids. One more morning swim. Doused and dunked again in the current, inky, my hair forgets its braid. In our loaded boat, we slip into the gentle Class II rapid below Thrifts Ferry, catch the eddy on river left. We move through the world, for a little longer, on our knees. In the morning mist, the Chattooga seems all the stranger now, even as I come to know it by sluice and bend and the stones bruising my foot. That's something the river has taught us: the greater the intimacy, the more evident the strangeness.

When the mist starts to clear, the sun strikes tassels of lichens hanging low in the trees. I mistakenly call them *sphagnum*, but "No," he tells me, "that's a ground moss. *Usnea* is what's in the trees." I say the name over and over to remember, "*Usnea, usnea*," knowing that, in time, I'll forget what those lichens are called and will simply love their nameless gray-green wisps bearding the branches that reach over the water as our small boat passes by.

SCREENPORCH AS PRAYER

HERE, INTERIOR MEETS EXTERIOR, THRESHOLD between kitchen scent and a wind murmured with skunk. Screen blocks June bugs and bats though not the slant rain. There is a little time. Metal washtub harbors nasturtium and petunia, and here, the boots to pull on when ready. I tweeze five ticks off the dog, suffocating them first in Vaseline. Yesterday, she snagged a bunny from under the hosta and, the day before, massacred the new robins. Her murderous face spoking bird legs, her hind leg trembling. She sprawls now to my touch. Board fitted and mesh tacked to make space for mercy. And this heat—let the sky make use of it. Out here, I read a letter from my brother who, last year, put that turnbuckle on the screen door to lift its drag and who has loved his wife for twenty years. He's building some chairs out of cherry and teaching his son our country's dark truths. *Letters slow life down,* he writes. I picture him calling forth the deeper cherry grain with Minwax finish and filling out the shapes outlined for us that seemed so large, capacious, and demanding when we were small enough to fit in closet forts and snug vests with snaps. P.S.—he doesn't remember that summer I asked him about, when we went to the demolition derby. But I remember his friend Jack's name called on the loudspeaker and the blue raspberry snow cones in the stands and our disposition toward homesickness. He is, I think, a good father to his son. A good teacher at the community college. Good husband.

May the chairs turn out. He prays for me in his hot-kernel heart to know what shape my life. I water dog and nasturtium and hear my mother's thoughts on the governor over the phone, my sister's talk of graduate school, my friend's news of her dad dying. And the radio, bad news all around from Yemen, Detroit, the local high school.

On the table, the market Cherokee Purples and Brandywines ripen, two nectarines and a newspaper boat of blue lake beans for my love. Out here, in these two chairs, was our beginning when we said I miss your shape when you're not near, I his shape of a single dad doing his best, trim beard shaved neck smell of sandalwood soap but stronger smell of lakewater, filling my hallway, shirtsleeves rolled up and shoulders to knead and to help brace me, and he my shape of whatever it is. I know it only to be a shape of something not yet final.

Please, God, a little more time before I go. I promise I'll be ready. After a bit, I won't really need the screen so intact. See here, this corner is already loose and I've left it unrepaired, and a few bats get in. I put my cheek down upon the porch floor, my temple, my heavy hair, and feel the flutter of a wing.

AS IF ALREADY ALWAYS

I PLANTED A WISTERIA SEED HE FOUND ON THE TRAIL YESTERDAY. I put the pot on a tile on the radiator to get morning sun because you never know and I love wisteria vine. Everything is already present in a seed, they say. Like a womb with all its eggs from birth, like that moment on the river in June when I'd seen about all the rhododendron I could stand, and then some, in all stages at once—the browned petals fallen in the eddies, the pert blooms along the bank, the tight buds still lousy with *almost*. Like when we are about to slip sluiceward in the tandem boat, no one watching, and just before we load in, in the right-before-the-rush-of-water, he might kiss my ear, and in that *before* is everything and always, a moment kernelled with all our possibilities—the looking for a house or pricing building supplies, how many rooms and acres; the windfall kindling in the washtub; cornbread mounding the cast iron; the kids' confusing science homework; and the aging; and the fittedness of aging together.

The yes is simple even though it's complicated by our lack of confidence in marriage and the sudden court decision that awards him full custody of his kids two weeks after we meet. *As if already always* wrote my friend Devon when I wrote her about him. And I told him, the first time we made love, it felt like home. Also the last time, yesterday, as it rained. What did I mean? Home, perhaps, for our younger and meaner and more wayward selves, and for the hopeful selves too, the possible future selves with good ideas for supper—I think pork loin and biscuits. Maybe the next years will look wholly different than this, maybe they will not even be shared. But I can only say it feels like home, and home is a place where all your selves come running.

ONCE, IN DUBLIN, I SAW the Diego Velázquez painting *Kitchen Maid with the Supper at Emmaus*. Clay bowl on clay bowl like music softly filling the National Gallery of Ireland. A maid with hands that seem smooth when wet, her hair wrapped in white rhyming with pitcher, garlic bulb, rag (or is it spice paper?), and the faint corona in the upper left-hand corner. The maid listening, like someone who, as a child, heard clay hit surface like a bell rung, mortar and pestle like chimes, bread rising in susurration. Some people hear music everywhere. It's a matter of recognition. One hand on the pitcher, the other at rest. She does not reach for the rag (I think it's a rag). Maybe she is listening to the bread breaking.

A tiny supper is shared by a tiny resurrected Jesus and two people in the upper left corner, one of them out of the frame but for a wee gesturing hand. The maid and her shadow and worktable fill the foreground. She was painted in early seventeenth-century Seville, so possibly an enslaved woman was the model. Another version of the painting, maybe a copy, which hangs in Chicago and is called simply *Kitchen Scene*, features the maid and her workspace only, no whiff of religious narrative in the corner, though still the attentive tilt of her head, listening, caught in a moment of overhearing everything. I might prefer that version which leaves what she hears, her attunement, more secret and less scripted. Not even Velázquez hears what she hears, knows what she knows. And maybe she's not eavesdropping at all but, instead, hearing a thing meant for her.

NO KITCHEN MAID IS MENTIONED IN THE EMMAUS STORY OF THE BIBLICAL TEXT. Her wrapped hair goes unnoted. In the Gospel of

Luke, right after Jesus is killed and buried, two grievers, Cleopas
and an unnamed other, walk the road to Emmaus, west of Jerusa-
lem. A stranger, who is really the newly risen Christ, joins them.
He remains anonymous to the men as they walk, even when they
tell him their grief and he peels it open, like a fruit. Or maybe they
are not both men; my brother mentioned to me he thinks they are
husband and wife since in John's Gospel, at the foot of the cross,
the company of women includes *Mary the wife of Clopas*, an alter-
native spelling. It makes sense that it's a couple because when they
want to keep this stranger close they say, Stay, come home with us,
to the blanketed pallet. Stay and fill the room with your talk, and
here the maid brings you tea with milk.

It's not until he sits at their table, blesses the bread and breaks
it, that they realize who he is. At the point of their recognition, he
vanishes. But not before he had his hands on bread again. Maybe
it was raining and he smelled the rain, maybe the tea was minty or
sweetened, maybe the kitchen maid knew right when he darkened
the door, from the gamy whiff of him. Knew he was someone who
had put his head down into the wind, here in this in-between, after
rising from the dead, before leaving the world altogether.

I'M ALWAYS DRAWN TO THESE GOSPEL SCENES from the reputed
forty days between resurrection and ascension when Jesus is hard
to recognize. Drawn again to the first scene when, mistaken for the
gardener, he calls the name of Mary Magdalene outside his tomb
and she almost drops her jar of burial spices. Here, in another
scene, he cooks breakfast fish upon a driftwood fire. In another, he
invites doubtful Thomas to touch the fleshy holes in his palms and
between his ribs. The Jesus in these scenes is in that strange crevice
of time when he still wants to hold things and raise up his hands
so the breeze can whistle through the punctures, as if someone has
made an instrument of him. He still wants to share supper, even
if he is on the other side of death, and I can't blame him for that.

The New Testament writers cited these post-resurrection appearances as proof, so the messianic story could not be denied, but it seems to me that, in these moments, Jesus is only trying to give himself time to gather up all his selves before giving in to invisibility, the stuff of spirit. He lingers in the good taste of bread and the feel of it broken, and here come running all his deathward, dead, and deathless selves. Here is the self from some time before Time, shaping substances into bleak beautiful sky and sea, demarcating moose from bear from long-haired human. Here his infancy and adolescence, here he's wiping feet and riding a foal, here his hand at the lathe. And then the executed one, and now some kind of eerie corona shine the Old Masters will always paint in white gypsum.

I don't think he had a home in this forty-day interstice. Only left hand and right hand wrinkled up, puckered around the wounds, flesh like a soft torn dishrag, holding bread. She saw, surely the maid knew it—he was home right then, in that moment flush with all his million selves, before he was gone. *Didn't our hearts burn when he was talking with us on the road?* she heard the couple say at the table in his shimmery wake when the rain then came in earnest.

I THINK: LET'S MAKE SOME egg salad sandwiches and make for the trail and swimming hole; I think: lift my dress. And we do; he does. I love his beard scruff, his kind single-parent-tired eyes, his read-aloud voice. His foraged morels and chanterelles, the salvaged pristine buzzard skull and intact rattler skin and feathers. Though we had just met, he gave me a heron's tail feather the first day he saw his children after the long custody battle and brought them home. They wept that day, and so did he, but they settled by his side as he began to tell them stories made from nothing with endings he didn't know until they revealed themselves. We fell in like pups, all four on the couch, laptop propped on Tolkien and medicinal plant guides and old *Harper's* issues for the next episode of

Lost in Space, which always became a few episodes after which they still sleepily asked him for a story. I would sometimes lie down and listen too, his voice like creek water. Then I'd stay or slip home, a twenty-minute drive away, to my hound and my tidy rooms.

I think our composite selves into a shared home, which could very well mean a small farmhouse amid some trees with deep enamel sinks full of paint brushes. My orderly spice drawer and alphabetized books, his unkempt gear room in which he can locate his fastidiously kept trout flies. Lemon balm leaves brewing tea in a jar set in the sun, some child we may have together that will go on and cry its cry and be named Simone or Moe or Gingerbug. Or home could mean the two of us together building bed frames for his children and all the beautiful laundry hung which matches the size of their preteen bodies, which will spend half the time with us, the other half with their mother, the custody now shared. I'd cut sprigs of sumac and bittersweet for an empty bottle on our table. I would pencil-sketch the bouquet to filigree and sew sequins to the sketch, glue on some beads and all his found feathers as a frame.

Home could mean these things, or it could mean something not at all ours, or mine. It could mean none of these things and still mean everything.

OF COURSE THEY RECOGNIZED HIM IN THE BREAKING OF BREAD, and the one who baked the bread to be broken indeed knew all along. The maid knows bread better than anyone in its singsong crypt. She knows the yeast, the rye or spelt, she knows that the crust is meant to be broken. She grinds the grain on the saddle quern with the handstone, the clay bowl a tomb for flour water oil herb, the leaven rising with plainest miracle in the dark dust under a towel. Her small daily resurrections in the fired oven. These are gestures she can make in her sleep, the music of clay things scoring her dreams.

And Jesus was talking to her, too, wasn't he? Right up until he disappeared and left Clopas and Mary dazed. The maid doesn't pick up the rag in the painting (or maybe it is in fact a wrapper that held spices), only keeps a hand on the white pitcher, but she will at some point take a rag to clean up when the two go outside in the rain, looking in the bushes for the vanished one with their hearts on fire. The music will tremor, clay on clay stacked, with morsels scattered, and the lips that were there on the cup will still be picturably pink. She'll be the only one left in the room by the table of her broken bread, standing in the shadow and the lamplight, somehow moved to a deeper love for her own story.

THIS MORNING HE IS CLEANING HIS HOUSE, BLASTING THE STONE PONEYS, Linda Ronstadt on vocals, traveling to the beat of her different drum. He texts me the Spotify link. With Linda you are less likely to curse the hair and Lego men in the drain or the stubborn stains in the toilet. In my own house I do some of the kids' laundry and find their candy wrappers and old gum in the dryer, and I think: what's it like to tend a fever of a child that yesterday ran through the woods and ate a ginger chew? Would I know this if we shared a home? He and I look on Zillow and Realtor.com now and then, text links, decide it's far too complicated to buy a place together, then text more links. Sometimes we simply imagine ourselves in the ranch or the Craftsman, or in the one with a barn with horse stalls, though we have no horses.

CLOPAS AND MARY KNEW EVEN IF THEY DIDN'T YET *KNOW*. They said, *Didn't our hearts burn when he was talking with us on the road? As he opened the truth to us, peeled it like a fruit?* They could sense already his alwaysness. Recognition is underneath somewhere, or amid, and it must be unsheafed, and it's always different than you thought. Our hearts respond to more than we can understand. Like how Susan Brind Morrow, in *The Dawning Moon of the Mind*, her book on the Pyramid Texts, says the meaning of poetry *is sig-naled as a glimpse of the active hidden layers of reality.* Just a glimpse of the secret workings. Jesus spoke more in poetry than prose, more in parable than homily. He dropped hints. The kingdom is a mustard seed, he said, and in a seed is everything. *It is the small-est of all seeds, but when it has grown it is larger than all the garden plants and becomes a tree, so that the birds of the air come and make nests in its branches.*

The kitchen maid knows the next one by heart: *The kingdom of heaven is like leaven that a woman took and hid in three measures of flour, till it was all leavened.*

I TRY TO HELP WITH HIS SON'S SCIENCE LESSON on independent and dependent variables. The boy reads the problem aloud and fidgets with a gear from something he's taken apart. The problem involves fertilizer, will it turn the bushes a deeper color and how much is needed.

"I don't know the dependent variable," he says.

"I don't either," I say. We are at his house. I pull the pizza from the oven. We take ball gloves and a ball which loosens talk, the plotlines of the *Lost in Space* episodes I've missed. "Just go ahead and tell me the end," I say when he's describing a robot-attack episode too scary for me to watch.

I think: I'm ready to help with science homework. Even if I don't really help because science is confusing to me, but I love to work together to fill in the orderly worksheet where there is a space for each answer though the answers elude us. I love how science is one of those fields that contains everything in it, us and our pizza and our atoms bouncing around. This is what home means, what it is.

I'M FASCINATED BY THAT PART WHEN JESUS DISAPPEARS, poof, as if he's too welled up with everything to bear being contained in the small room any longer. Maybe the maid turned and watched the vanishing. Did it look like a rupture in space, or a glitch, or a half-second blip of a black hole? I think it might have been so complicated a vision that it was actually simple, pared back to the starkness of winter woods, starting her over in a place where she could see her breath. Here is each stone on the steep hillside and each handhold-sapling and the sheer light right before dusk when the sun gets brighter, then is gone. I love the brightening before the gone. He was holding the bread, then he went bright, then—

LAST WEEK, HE AND I went to meet a realtor to look at a house. Off-grid, solar panels and a generator, surrounded by national forest. But the road had six creek crossings and we had just gotten a hard rain. His Subaru made it through the first three and we hoped the water didn't reach the engine, but we parked and waded across the next two in rainboots. The sixth crossing was running too high and too fast, so we had to turn back and never saw the house with its deck and pond and beautiful wood floors pictured in the online listing. I reasoned that it was just as well, we wouldn't have been able to drive to work sometimes, too much anxiety for me. Lousy internet options probably, iffy cell signal. But seven acres and roaming bears and room enough for him and me and the kids. And a room for us to write in and for a guest's bed. And a creek nearby to play in and watch flood its boundary. It sounded like a dream. Sometimes you get a feel for a house right away, a home-feel—yes, this is a place where cornbread will mound golden, where you can easily forgive the hen its shit on the porch swing—so if we just could have *seen* it, we could have known. But we were cold and soaked up past our knees so we headed back and said, There will be others.

We tucked into his house, the kids with their mother, heated up beef barley soup with sourdough, laid a fire in the grate. He set up two camping chairs on the kitchen tile so we could dry our bones, thigh to thigh, and share a beer. The firelight flickered across his mantel clutter—books of poems and shorebird taxonomies, the cobwebbed mirror, his son's linocut print. We slept like spoons in this home he rents, a place both solid and temporary at once. In truth, it felt almost good to let the real estate gem go since there was something vivid in simply fording the creek in our boots and taking each other's hands when it got deep.

I THINK JESUS WAS GATHERING his many selves in those forty days because, for the rest of eternity, wouldn't he be invisible except in paintings? A couple millennia of incorporeality have already accumulated. Does he ever look out over it all with a kind of homesickness? What he'd give for hot cornbread with butter. Slab of bacon. To handle it with his dishraggy hands. I love that his wind-instrument torso remained speared though maybe not gory-looking in the resurrected afterlife, a healed scar but not an eradicated one, so that doubtful Thomas could open the soft wound as if opening a letter. Doesn't that suggest that resurrection includes everything, all the selves good and gathered, fulfilled in their story, none annulled? Was he trying to show us how to love our stories no matter what?

I WAS REREADING A LITTLE BOOK that fits in a dress pocket, *Mystical Hope*, another by the priest Cynthia Bourgeault, and I found beautiful her interpretation of *apocatastasis*, a theological doctrine which means, in brief, a final restoration of things to a blessed state at the end of time. When treated in depth by the likes of Gregory of Nyssa and Origen of Alexandria, the doctrine handles the end of days and what happens to evil souls and how to bring them back to the fold and so forth. But in Bourgeault's small book, it means something different, something closer to this definition of home as a place teeming with your multiple selves. She writes that, in this restoration, time is held in the big bowl of Mercy itself, Mercy as a space, and the space grows wide enough to contain all potentials. *In that Mercy all our history—our possible pasts and possible futures, our lost loved ones and children never born—is contained and fulfilled in a wholeness of love from which nothing can ever possibly be lost. It is not a vision we can stand too long in the presence of.* It is also a vision that helps me understand why the yes is simple.

AND MAYBE THAT'S WHAT MY FRIEND DEVON MEANT when she scrawled *as if already always.* Love—Mercy—as a trustworthy and inevitable container of everything, even not-love; a moment kernelled with all possibilities, even the ones untapped. Maybe that's why the outcome doesn't matter so much, all this business of partner and children and marriage and cohabitation and children's future science projects and a dreamy off-grid A-frame in the woods—it's all simply a window looking out. Or a tutorial, once again, in the subject of desire, for how many times must I learn that fulfillment already breathes within longing itself and breathes even more deeply in longing relinquished, that the eternal thrums in time, and abundance is found in the meager stalk? That the end is seeded right there in the beginning.

Just now, he comes back from paddling Johns Creek, swollen with spring rain, and giddily brings me bone-white sheds he found, a lucky nine-point set of antlers a whitetail had dropped in the plain open instead of losing it to the usual snarl of thicket. And I think: yes, I have all this, the solid and temporary simple sheds in my hands and the solid and temporary bearded face that I kiss in gratitude for the gift.

No matter what happens, it's a foretaste of the greater Mercy that holds us, this coming to love one another's stories, this experience of home in our togetherness, where all my selves, out of breath, come racing like kids in a summer night game. Here's the girl drawing feathers with pastels in junior high art class, the bookish teen at the demolition derby, the woman once married to a man who drew her fallen asleep reading before the woodstove with twelve shapes he called consolations painted white over her sketched head. Here's the me who still pines for a woodstove and has to let go of the A-frame because the creek is impassable, but who doesn't let go of her stubborn willingness to risk love again, as if risking it for the first time, with this man who takes her to a tributary of the James River deep enough to skinny-dip in the light lucking through the August canopy. And here are so many selves I hope to still become before I die, and maybe after. In an email today my mother said she wants to swim more and grow her hair long before she dies. Me too. Long-haired fishlike selves. I wonder, does he feel, in my love for him, his prolific selves all welcomed? I hope so.

BUT SHE IS THE ONE I CAN'T HELP DREAMING ABOUT, the kitchen maid. The enslaved one she was modeled on, the person she became in oils on canvas, listening, and the other versions of her and her story that only she knows. This version in the painting is the only one I know, and I love the folds on her headwrap, the white towel spilling from the basket hanging from a nail on the wall. I wonder about her simple yes to a lover, despite the complications. I wonder whether she wants a child to send off to and pick up from school and take out for a walk in the woods to crumble old corn-bread for the juncos. Or whether there might be children nearby and love for them is enough, more than enough. Or whether she's had her fill of child-rearing altogether. What kind of life does she make once the table is empty, the bread long broken, the Christ vanished, and the electric air all static around her? Mostly I won-der—what exactly does she hear right before that, in the moment of the painting, alert at her worktable, in the midst of clay on clay? Maybe the entire pageant is really about her story, how she hears the sudden sound of her many selves rushing, about to come round the corner.

ONCE, LITTLE LION

COME DARK, WE'LL LET THE MAPLE WATER COOL IN THE POT, sugar
it down to syrup in the morning. Go hang your lake-wet things
from the rafter and pull on your nightdress, your brother his pants
with frogs on them. Your hot head eased down like a sunfish back
into water. You ask again for a nightlight, afraid of the dark. It is
spring, the light is late. We want to take you both by canoe to sleep
by the river, you the daughter and son of my love and his first wife.
Smooth stones, the boxwoods. The cypress and green ash, and
there your tent—picture it. The light is late but not forever, you
protest, eventually the darkness will fall. But, I say, the dark settles
like the feathers of a great bird. Let's go by boat to camp where you
can hear the river all night though you do not see it. Though I am
not your mother, I will be there.

—The light is late but not forever.

But you have lived the day in lion form, in a dress handed
down. And see? See how the dark comes through the window
screens to cool our heads and bellies in your father's household as
we dream atop our beds. And see how only the dark unfolds the
luna moth like a letter, green-furred, little halogen far-come-near
to your bedside reading lamp.

—The light is late but not forever.

But we will build a driftwood fire, and when the embers cool
to nothing, we'll switch on our headlamps, slip into our tents to

glow them into globe lanterns. Then, lights out, you will hear the dark's feathers settling at last. Tailfeathers curled and dusty, each shaft tucked into shaft then fanned to cool. The moon not yet risen. If only you can come to love it—

ONCE, I ALSO FEARED THE DARK. The lamp snuffed, I feared the bat's wing brushing, the immense unknown swallowing my small knowable lit sphere. In my twenties, I read the German poet Rainer Maria Rilke, who composed the first poems of his *Book of Hours* also in his twenties, writing, all nerves and music, at the turn of a new century now old. He wrote them near Berlin, quick and intense, in the morning and evening, these *inner dictations*, he called them, written like a breviary. With such poems unspooling around him, he wrote in his journal in November 1899: *I have begun my life.* Here, the dark is fruit, is possibility. *You, darkness, of whom I am born*, he writes. *I love you more than the flame / that limits the world / to the circle it illumines / and excludes all the rest.* True, the light makes certain what wing or whatever brushes by. Yet it is not certainty we crave but softness. And embrace: *the dark embraces everything...lets me imagine / a great presence stirring beside me.* I prayed his breviary, I switched off the light, my mind hummed. You, darkness, I said. I clear a table for you. I drink to you, the anise-burn in my throat—here, a carafe of wine and a plate of bread. I open my screenless window to bats or whatever.

ONCE, IN THE DARK, VILLAGE WOMEN took the Orthodox icons from the slate-roof churches and hid them from this empire and that, under beds and in cellars, in the dung heap. In the folds of their dresses until the fires passed. I can tell you I saw the salvaged. I went to Greece to see what the darkness had protected, walked the road lined in oleander to the inland village of Theologos on the island of Thassos in the North Aegean Sea. I climbed the path to the stone and tile church of Agia Paraskevi, its clock tower plastered white, and inside: the gathered icons long hidden under beds and among root vegetables and buried—those archangels and saints women had hidden under their housedresses.

One icon was set apart: *Virgin & Child,* pre-Byzantine, made of wax and mastic in the sixth century, the priest told me, by the Apostle Luke, asking to be touched now, the deep lines in her headscarf ridged and raised like braille. I could imagine the Virgin's headscarf a nimbus glowing secret under crinoline. Some brave village girl whose heart did not stutter, did not hesitate as she swiped the raised waxen faces from their frame and fled, tucked them into horsehair skirts, safe sheaves of night. Climbed the hill, loving her own pulse, her own breath, knowing by feel the grove of trees in the dark. She settled her dress like feathers around her, whispering the secret she knew of the Holy One—darkness is not dark to you, just another shade of star.

LET ME TELL YOU ANOTHER STORY: Once, walking back from the church of stone and tile to the small blue house I was sleeping in near the sea, I saw an old man bring his TV out to the night porch for the soccer match. Shirtless, white tuft of hair in the glow. Mexico scored on Germany, the underdog victor, and he cheered like crazy then switched off the TV and sat in the dark for a long while. Somehow, I could sense his life come up in his throat, the goal he scored for his school, the girl, the motorbike, the country poor for growing things but a hydrangea bed for her. Cooled in the sweet dark remembering. He sat there long after I entered my rented house.

ONE NIGHT, YOU WILL PACK your small duffel, glimpse the crescent moon through the hung wet things, follow the road lined in oleander, led by moonlight then by nothing. The bat will want only to kiss you and pass. You will be lonely. The goats, once you leave the road for their path, will yield to you. Your heart like a country poor for growing things and then, one day—young olive groves and fig.

IN THE DARK SEA UNDER A DARK SKY you'll not braid your hair, nor even tie it, and how it will spread like inky wings in seawater. If only you can come to love it—

IN THE DARK, SOMEONE WILL leave pears by your door. We hope to take you by boat. It is spring. In the middle of the night maybe I will slip out of the tent I share with your father and find you sitting on the bank, listening to the river rapid you do not see. And though I am not your mother, I'll picture you years from now, sitting facing the sea as the goat bells start up in the night, your hair sea-wet. I'll not be there then, nor your father, nor your mother. But all of us will trust you to the embrace of the dark. Those pears, a few apricots—you will find them come light.

III.

WHEN OXEN DREAM OF OXEN

My yoke is easy, and my burden is light.

—Gospel of Matthew 11:30, English Standard Version

Unrecorded Gospel: "I watched," she says to him. "Something squirmed toward being," she says, "and I put my hand to the great hot side and could feel the unborn turn his soft nosebone as rudder, guiding his way out into the barn light." The woman is his friend, she is the teamster's daughter. She is speaking of the two oxen, one bull, one she-ox, a cow that calved not long ago and, now, after weaning, has returned to the yoke.

He watches the pair of beasts out the window. The man has not yet learned to hold the sadness of others or take on their shadows. This story goes back long before he keeps the dead from dying and dunks the leper in the river to raise him up with the skin of a baby. He is young. He watches the oxen nodding as they plod, as if they're saying yes to the morning. Mist still hangs haunting the hillside perimeter of the field where they drag the blade. The yoke presses across the considerable humps which rise over their forefeet, and the plow is heavy in its drag.

How the man met her: When, in his taciturn ways, he stood at the roadside a stranger, the teamster's daughter simply came to fetch him and gave him cake, had him sit at her table, her face odd and lovely. In time, they became friends, though she will not show up on the official record. She often watched his thin arms in the town square as he threaded the crowd and threw off the uncreative doctrines, like woolen cloaks; he wrestled them off, and she imagined him as a child waking hot from a nap, his small body a fist of sweat in his crib sheets. He is still younger than she, with an excess of everything, too much to fit inside. And he is still choosing his tutelage—where to place his hand to learn, to summon, to alter? Perhaps that's why she speaks of the calf, her hand pressed to the hot hide that day. She wonders whether his mother blew on his eyelids to wake him, whether he bolted upright and snapped to attention in that practiced way in which the gentle keep their gentleness hid because they do not yet understand it.

ALL THE ONIONS HUNG, THE beans soaking, the zinnia seeds gathered and cilantro gone feral—I'm finished now with the useless thinking. I have little time for thinking at all: I'm barefoot in a cold snap in June with hardly time enough to gather my mind and shoes before we spoon out the yams forgotten in the coals overnight and we're off in the car with my gazpacho chilled, with his quinoa and salmon and lemon, with his children from his other life, heading out to watch, from a high place, the storms roll in. The two kids stand there sighting thunderheads soberly, mist pillows into the Blue Ridge. The bodies of these children not mine whom I love are unflinching, growing, full of questions.

Because of them and because of the sad, stratified desert-world they will inherit from us, I am done wasting time on thought that doesn't take me through to the other side of itself, done with poems not ancient enough to take me into a time more present than the present. Give me instead a thought like the soil rolling black unto the plow to yield up seashells embedded in the stones sparking against the blade. This furrow in the seabed, these ox hoofprints on the shore, and the Virginia pines all going to madrone with red bark like peeled skin.

As soon as we have thought something, Simone Weil writes, *try to see in what way the contrary is true.* As desert stretches to desert and human suffering reveals the insufficiencies in our care for one another, I seek thoughts trembling in tension with their contraries, for maybe there is hope in the contrary: thoughts of freedom and obligation, burden and ease, gravity and light. Take first the simplest thought of gravity's curse, the weight around our mortal necks. Take first this body.

Here in middle age, he and I have busted parts in us. At midlife, one can no longer deny the press: yoked to earth by gravity, yoked to the meat of the flesh and its various needs, rashes, chafing, scabs and chigger bites; base with basic hungers, our defecations, routines of blood, sore backs and thinning hair and skin showing the drag. And laden, most heavily, with our failures. How often we bow to the ground in defeat or in desperate need of a stretch. But *Gravity is grace,* writes Wendell Berry. *All that has come to us / has come as the river comes, / given in passing away.* Berry writes the ancient-new kind of poems. So, there is gift in this gravity, he says, a gift we receive in no other way than by submitting to its force. As a woman who bears the mark of gravity in sagging body, *I possess by loss / the earth I live upon / and stand in and am. The dark / and then the light will have it.*

What we have, what we are, then, is what we have lost, we the stones smoothed by the river and left on the cobble bar for the taking. Sometimes I pray a blessing over the dreams dreamt in the man I love, my companionable beast of gravity, over his humble hopes for this day, that he may brew his kids a good batch of ginger ale with lemon balm and elderflower. That he and I may be able to do the useful thinking. There is time now for only our best thinking. Soon our muscles will be the stuff of moths and our organs the gases of stars. I am grateful for the hours lying side by side, I in his T-shirt. The side-by-side easing our heaviness.

WB: *In work of love, the body / forgets its weight.*

"IT WAS A GOOD DAY," says the woman to him, "the day I watched the calving." Her bright blue shift has darts at the bust, and she is beautiful in her hiddenness. *Peahen*, he thinks, for no real reason, *peahen asleep in the tree,* though the hens are drab and do not wear the wild peacock color of the dress. This morning at her table she gives him honeyed semolina cake with dates, with almonds, though she has little.

Her face is warm, olive, tired. She touches her black untied hair and might flee her life if she could, circle, boundless, above the unpainted tiles and clay pots and open windows through which the gee-and-haw of her father wafts. Yet the young man senses, within her leafy inchoate desires, she would not flee. Her heart's excess spills into the sink—she, too, understands excess—and onto the sill where shells rest in her special arrangement.

She feels his creativity swimming and diving and embroidering itself in rapid stitching, like the tiniest of leaps enormous with color. She knows that, at this point, he can merely suggest; he is still a man with no language in common with the others. He can only gesticulate, shape what he sees with the birdlike signs of his hands all knuckle and joint. He makes silk like a worm with his hands, idea-silk.

Everyone asks him questions impossible to answer except obliquely, except with a sly gaze gone wayward to the potted rosemary. They say, What are you afraid of? for it seems he is afraid to answer, but it's simply that the dry rosemary's fragrance is sharpest when its tiny leaves are broken. Also, he does not yet *know* the answer, except that it is as unlikely as it is inevitable. Except that it is something infinitely small. He is still learning. He is still young; this his friend understands. She is waiting for him to be changed into himself.

His eyes trail the oxen framed in the screenless window by

the white of the wall, in their bondage and subjection—nod, nod, plod, huge heaving noses. Soft gee, soft haw, calling. The teamster's goad is wholly unneeded now, for the beasts are old and so accustomed. They seem to the young man bulky automatons. They will pull through the morning hours and into the day's heat, this team of Brahman, a breed that can sweat to cool themselves. These are the oxen of the poor, surviving on meager feed. Hitched before dawn, right out the low door of their stalls, they can go all day, with lucky long ears to swat the flies. Two bulls are best, but one of the team is female because, though a cow is weaker, it's multipurposed for the poor—can take the yoke, be bred, calve, give milk. *How much you can ask of a body*, he thinks.

I TELL HIM I AM WRITING AGAIN ABOUT OXEN, that there is something I need to learn from them, and he teases that I am indeed more ox than feline. It's true. I'd rather take up a chore than most anything. I'm drawn to the head down, heart a carburetor, the blade dragged, a hillside mist and some barking love of morning labor.

There is also something spiritually attainable there. I cannot, it seems, in these middle years, be again the tree I once was in my youth, as from the first Psalm, the tree that shall not be moved, planted by the waters that bringeth forth sweet fruits, whose leaf shall not wither. Faith so firm and anchored, roots drinking from the hidden silvered aqueducts somehow moonshot and clean. But maybe I can be the ox tethered to that tree, laying my great face to the moss greening its north side.

Also, down where the oxbow is fitted might I find some useful thoughts on freedom and obligation, burden and ease, gravity and light?

The she-ox returns me to Simone Weil again, returns me to her *Gravity & Grace*, its aphorisms like braided smoke. Weil sings always in my head discordantly, if you can call it singing. I want the utter discord and to be changed by it.

Weil: *Love is not consolation, it is light.*

If we want a love which will protect the soul from wounds we must love something other than God.

Weil as a she-ox herself was yoked to no one, so yoked to everyone, as slave, as astringent angel, severe harlequin in color patches sewn from rags. I want to cup her thin bovine face, the face she wore all her brief life. Her breath heavy, eternity blowing in and out of her, she the bellows.

Love is not consolation, it is light. I want to ask her: can it not be both? A salve and a laser beam. Can I not curve around Weil's saintly angular body like a plush blanket, the kind his kids sleep cocooned in? I have lost all my hard edges, prefer to not sleep alone, prefer to grocery shop with children in mind, to feel the forehead for fever abating. Yet I am her disciple still.

I believe she'd be open to this bothness: *try to see in what way the contrary is true.*

On the matter of gravity, she writes: *What is the reason that as soon as one human being shows he needs another (no matter whether his need be slight or great) the latter draws back from him? Gravity.*

Gravity's force something different here than in WB's poem; here, it's the central Darwinian law of human action—to exercise power when you have it, to preserve self, to protect one's face from every blow. It's the natural law. And what is the opposite? What is weightlessness?

Weil thinks through to the other side, to the strange law: *To come down by a movement in which gravity plays no part... Gravity makes things come down, wings make them rise: What wings raised to the second power can make things come down without weight? ... Grace is the law of the descending movement.*

Grace is the goodness of down, to not draw back from another's need but shoulder it. A kind of weightlessness other than we expect, for it sinks, yields, bows.

There's a dog-eared passage that I return to most often: *For the*

afflicted the one and only road to faith is through the virtue of spiritual
poverty. But this is a cryptic truth. For spiritual poverty appears to
resemble resignation to slavery. And it is indeed almost identical with
it, except for an infinitely small difference. We are always brought back
to something infinitely small, which is infinitely more than everything.

What is the small distinction? She seems to urge us to drudgery
and shackles though we long for and esteem flight and freedom,
and it is indeed *almost* drudgery, except that the burden is carried
like a thing weightless, a sack of feathers. Except we can choose the
goodness of down. To her, the opposite of resignation isn't escape
from the oxbow but knowing the oxbow to be a garland of flowers.

Sometimes I pray a blessing over Weil, the patron saint of contraries, of otherwise, of distinctions. I scribble on scraps of paper
the kind of blessings she might hold in her fist:

You homeless will be a carriage of bones like a crisp nut hull
sheltering light.

Today may it be the barren woman whom all the children ask
for watermelon and witness.

Into your glacial despair will the bluebells come, in the stand
of birch the belled blue groan of cracking ice.

The day asks you to go fetch the mail and go easy down this
road, asks nothing but everything.

THE WOMAN'S FACE IS WARM, OLIVE, TIRED. He thinks again: *Pea-*
hen asleep in the acacia tree. All her feathers settled and soft. There
are contours he sees beneath the dress rise and fall. She tells him
the oxen have nearly aged past use. She is not sure her father can
afford another pair, he has sold the new calf and spent that. She
lights the stove to heat water for tea and sleepily talks, says that
when they were fresh—the bull newly cut, castrated into docility,
and the heifer not yet pregnant by another steer with any of her
eight calves to come—she was a small girl watching when their
cloven hooves were each shoed with two half-moons. She felt the

oxen's names on her tongue, single-syllable and longer, near-side, off-side, Lark and Luther. She put her ear to the cow's side, then to the bull's, to hear the expressive body, how the many stomachs worked. Later, so quietly in Lark, she could hear the first folded-up quiver of a calf becoming. When she was a girl, the teat filled her hand. She held the cow's big face in both palms and did not know how she was possible.

This quivery world so new to him, a carpenter, he knows joinery and lathe and grain. Out the window, the oxen pause in the shade of the cedar, the teamster gone somewhere. Ruminant chew of green, a tremor of dewlaps and a shake of the head near-side, off-side. The young man wants to touch them. His friend's back is turned. He rises silently from the table and moves like someone deciding to dance so to understand movement differently (same arms, legs, head, elbows, but it's *different*). He leaves her talk scattered on the floor tile, like a toss of jacks mid-play, leaves her kitchen while she is turned toward the flame.

Mist lingers on the hillside and drapes those aged almost past use, past surprise or uproar or buck. Here in the shade, given to the yoke, the oxen stand sturdily and, it seems to him, without intelligence, only dim, blocky minds ruined by servitude and habit. But is that what he really thinks? He notes mild tumors near the eyes in their faces acquiesced and downturned. No resistance left under oxbow and pin. Have they no memory of roaming with gangly legs, or of stupor, free, in the sun and sweetgrass? His own thin arms, languid and unbent at his sides, droop as if borrowing the oxen's tonnage. Why does he want to touch them? These with their gaze dulled to yellow? And yet. Where else to look but in the unlikely place? He has learned that much.

Also, there's a recent rending in his body. This propulsion upward toward orbit, lightness, outness as beyond the dark, but then another pull toward lying down unto the downward breeze, to sleep submerged, so heavily, beneath the weight of his own flesh. Or not to sleep but to tunnel bizarrely down and through, as one might grope toward caves where, in the depths of the volatile planet, there is perhaps greater light than that of the sun. He cannot yet make sense of the dissonant urges, he the importunate, open-mouthed, here in the shade with the beasts and the burden.

(In the kitchen of kitchen sounds, the woman stands barefoot on the single rug in her blue dress. Hand through her hair, and supposing him still at her table, she wonders about him, his folds, his equanimous yet restive eyes, his carpenter hands. She will turn and upbraid or touch him. She cups some of her excess and, as if ladling, pours it into the sink. When she turns from the basin with the rose tea prepared on the woven tray, with two slices of cheese, she thrills softly to find him gone.)

Under the cedar, their dewlaps quake, their noses rise, horns curve barely up, those pendulous ears swat absently at flies, and the yoke presses, even at rest. Their only-ness of life fills him with feeling. Lark the she-ox is shy to the human hand reaching out, but Luther snuffles his wet nostrils into the palm with apparent affection. Then the young man circles behind and wedges himself between the oxen still joined, as between two mounds of breathing mountain. And, as the teamster's daughter did once, he spreads out his fingers and places his hand to the great side of the still-but-still-heaving bull, there against the short-hair hide so hot and coarse.

All grows dark in the man's mind, not from any shade thrown by the cedar, but as if slipped forward or backward a notch in time, or in species. The darkness comes from the night in the late quiet barn, the place where the Brahmans cool themselves in separate stalls, unyoked. The first sense that the man senses is the smell the bull-ox smells, the milk-crust smell on the cow's udder a few weeks past weaning, a sweet residual rot, white and grime and chalk. The man is so aware of Lark but does not see her in her separate stall and is not near her but is so near her. He feels what it's like to be free of her body as the bull-ox readies to sleep. And the man anticipates according to reason: in the beast of burden's dream, won't there be a wide space of lush wilderness and won't the ox, alone and unhitched, finally know gusts of wind across his cooling hide? There will be a brook or a river, and groves of raining-down fruits, and the bull that lives with great austerity now, will he not dream himself in the pastures of Bashan and will he not be made fat and strong there, and fierce? And then—there will appear in the dream a place out in orbit among the far planets, where the unfettered beast in loose skin, all beyond the yank of gravity and the gee and the haw, will radiate weightlessness.

The sleepy bull feels a barn bat flutter at the nose, the eyelid, like a kiss, and then, as if obliging the man's request for the dream, the ox tucks his forefeet, his haunches, and sleeps.

PERHAPS THE GREATEST BURDEN WE BEAR IS DEATH, FOR WHICH THERE IS NO EASE. If I try to think to the other side of this thought, I meet the story of the unrestrained Author of Life funneled into a deathward body. The Godself becoming a set of cells and sensors and limitations, a young learning being: smallish hands held out probing the unnamed world, learning from it how to make metaphors for love, for truth. Learning to decipher light uttered in dawn's many tongues. The Word Made Flesh fumbling with seams and sticks, rushing in high grass, palm out, *this* and *this*. I think of the Word trying out words, at first clumsily. He sounds out the text unscrolled before him, one of dawn's languages written in beautiful beetle-footprints, while the touchable world around him serves as the azurite and vermillion illuminating the manuscript.

And what about touching and deciphering other flesh? To touch the beast is to know it as meat, as something that will die and give in to gravity. What might it have felt like for the Word from the Beginning, the Word with God that was God, a vast foamy fog of eternity, to put a hand to a heaving ark of flesh and those working stomachs and joints that would one day give out? To touch the beast's death and learn from it.

As I write this, I study Rembrandt's *Slaughtered Ox*, painted in 1655. The headless beast hangs in a dark basement of a butcher shop, tied up by its hind legs spread wide. Skinned and gutted and glowing. It's the wild generative glow that stuns me, light where there should be dark. Hélène Cixous writes us all into this painting: *We are standing in the cellar. The ox is a lamp, an enormous hanging lamp. It is the aster of this night. It irradiates. The ox is beautiful. The ox shines in the darkness.*

As I write this, the man I love calls on a night in November to say he's shot a deer. Will I help work up the meat? He tells me the story: a walk with his rifle with his kids, not much of the hunter's intent, but only if he happened to see one. There on the ridge. The kids cried a little for the death but were okay. He's slaughtered with them before, after all, as they were strapped to his chest in a sling when they were babies. He has cut out and handled the heart already. *The origin of prayer*, his friend told him, this kind of intimacy with meat, this gratitude in flesh handling flesh.

When I go over in old clothes with freezer paper and Ziplocs to help work up the venison, it's the light of the hanging buck body I see first. He has removed the head with the cordless reciprocating saw and spread a tarp beneath the carcass. He's inserted a stick between the hooves to hang it from the hook in the pavilion. November light streams from it. Severed head in the duff nearby, six-point rack, he will bury it and, next summer, dig it up bleached and cleaned by maggots to set on the mantel. His shirtsleeves rolled up, muck boots to the knee, blood on them. The body gutted but still some turds to clean out. He pulls the knife down the length of it to cut free the tenderloin in a single strip. Removes the fish lodged up in the chest between the forelegs.

At the table, with his knife, he shows me how to butterfly the backstrap. I cut winged hearts that will feed us when cooked into small medallions, feed the kids, all the morsels of wild berry and root that the deer ate, before the shot fired, flavoring the meat. Seems we can feel the beast running, see the blur of branches and rain, *possess by loss*, in Wendell B's words, this life. This knife has been sharpened. I could be seamstress or calligrapher for how focused I am with all of myself as I participate in this rite of sustenance. I can hear the tenderness of the flesh give way. At the other table, the kids scrape cartilage from the rib cage, poising their bodies as if over a complicated Lego set.

The origin of prayer. Something holy in the provision for their hungers. Something sharp in my memory of a deer in the barn, my brother's first buck, the stacked square bales we played on right next to it. His youth and boyhood steaming out from the hollow gut of the life lost.

Every so often, you're given to see yourself from the inside, in both crudeness and magnificence. *The ox is hurled to the bottom. And there are no angels,* writes Cixous. *We are this creature, which even turned upside down and decapitated and hung beneath the earth—when it is seen with those eyes that don't reject the below, that don't prefer the above—maintains its majesty.* I don't know that it's majestic, but it's vivid, the body seen this way, the *below* when it's thought through to its other side, to something beautiful. Our vulnerable, burdened selves, arm bones tied hook to hook and spread, give off strange light from here below. Think of God's palm put to the vessel of meat that we are, learning that peculiar brightness.

THE DREAM TAKES SHAPE WITH VAPOROUS HEAT, puzzling the man at the start, for the ox dreams the oxen together, the oxen yoked, as if dreaming a dawn with the same blade dragged. So, at first, it seems that the thick ash of servitude and familiarity has clogged even the dreams of the ox. The man is crestfallen: maybe they are shuttered simpletons after all, captive to habit and knowing no better and nothing else. Nothing to teach him. He feels a pull to return to his friend from this side of the dreamed world, picturing her as the peahen asleep and wanting now the rose tea and her face in the screenless window light.

But he will stay within the dream of bull and cow together, just a little longer. For as he looks more deeply, more closely, the cow grows these baby rosettes, blushy, behind her long floppy ears, like pretty decorations, and the bull is not a gray-mash color but becomes a deep nutty brown, with sharp black eyes—odd—as if the two are growing more beautiful together. And this one, the bull, always off-side, she near-side, makes a study of her intimate neck and, beneath the borne bar, the divot on her withers, her jawbone set then loosening, the yawn and yawn and wish, and the bull says to her: *It's you. There you are.*

As if he has been seeking her, the always-beside, as if she has been far away all this time.

The bull-ox thus explores her, perceiving her strange, this most-known one, dreaming her unknown and new, all the composite of her, near-side, now with strips of flesh like lace curtain hanging over her bones, now only her white bones melodic in the wind. Her flesh then retrieved, reknitted, he sees each rosette behind her flop of ear, the petal of the petal, and the mouth of her mouth, and the ease of her weight. The featherlight of her heaviness.

THIS IS OUR MIST DRAPING us. This your black wet snout, the scent of sweet oat straw still greened and half rotted from the broken bale, the secret on the other side of both of us aged. Bloody one of light, all the way inside you, down and through your many stomachs. You are big with sound, all your bones, your haunch, your hindfeet, hoof. Sometimes your sounds are buttery, other times like a humming yum of a child with cake and cream.

———

Peeling back an unruly love—

What I want is you and your good, in the mist hung on the hill rising at the end of our acre lot—we pull to the mist each day, we feel it on our faces, garland of flowers yokes us light as snow— and who are you and who are you here with me?

She, like a faceted gem, is conduit to wonder, vital and whole as a fruit, in the downward turn of the head and the neck, the beautiful being-with. A great ease is found there.

I think of transmutations of baled oat straw into cud into streams of living water into filament of light. Of fresh butter into orange creamsicle from the deep freeze, of stranger into kin. Of freedom into obligation into freedom. Maybe that's the beating heart of a dialectic: freedom *is* obligation, transformed; burden *is* ease, gravity *is* light. I sense this heartbeat in feeling bound to a son and daughter not mine, loving them beyond the boundaries between us, a not-mother as mother watching them watch the storms roll in from a great height, their cornsilk hair blustered by the wind.

Always when I've pictured a child I might have, there she is again on that blue bike like mine, delivering butter. Streamers from the handlebars, rainbow-spray, zooming across the same cattle guards I crossed when I sold butter for a dollar a package, butter churned from the cream skimmed from the milk of my family's Guernsey. Maybe I picture the child thus because this mountain landscape is where I began to learn the meanings of care for one another, of community, of freedom.

I understood as a child that a woman named Naomi was my neighbor because I delivered butter to Naomi—we pronounced her name *Nyomah*—and she turned from the window in her polyester dress, fetched a dollar from her purse and opened her deep-freeze to give me an orange creamsicle in a cellophane wrapper. That world in my tiny, rural enclave felt intact, the place where I could walk the loop and touch and name each parcel of land—I write about it often, that palpable togetherness. My first understanding of community as familiarity, the known, the same.

And there I also began to understand the idea of freedom as fleeing this familiar place, since it was a place said by many to squelch potential. Community was heavy and thick with habit, daughters living next door to mothers and grandmothers, same asphalt siding on the houses. A deep sense of belonging, stifling yet safe. Freedom was flight, elsewhere, personal success, a move to the Bay Area, to a high-rise. Scary maybe, but a relieving loss of accent and a cleanse of the smudge of kin that, back home, never left your skin. This is the forthright narrative of escape known to rural, poor places the world over.

Of course I did not read, back then, Weil and Rousseau and Kant and Heidegger, or participate in the philosophical debates over individualism, freedom, community, totalitarianism, though, like anyone, I participated in an existence conditioned by all that political philosophy in my little body carrying a sack of butter pats, loving and snipping sprigs of the invasive multiflora rose, sucking a creamsicle and treading my grooves in the terrain.

Community and freedom were two very separate words set out before me in the bald light with no shadows. In such a glare, we humans know well the impoverishment of either-or.

In *Terms of the Political*, Roberto Esposito, Rhiannon Noel Welch, and Vanessa Lemm dig into the roots of political language that's been hollowed out, words understood too straightforwardly in that bald, reductive light: *Every political concept,* they write, *has an illuminated part that is immediately visible, but also a dark zone, a cone of shade from which, only through contrast, such light bursts forth.*

Returning again to Weil: *As soon as we have thought something, try to see in what way the contrary is true.*

There are lush shadows in the word *community*; it holds its opposites. Esposito and Welch and Lemm write that, although we have such a long history of defining the word as *belonging, identity and ownership—that is, the community as something that identifies someone with his/her own ethnic group, land, or language—the originary term* community *has a radically different sense. One need only open a dictionary to learn that* common *is the exact contrary of* one's own; common *is what is* not *one's own, or what is unable to be appropriated by someone. It is what belongs to all or at least to many, and it therefore refers not to the same but to the other.*

A small aperture, then, in my childhood understanding: there is community not because we neighbor houses, have the same talk and points of reference, but more so because of something about butter and creamsicle, feeding a body not mine and the other doing likewise; relinquishing what belongs to me, even my certainties, when I bear witness to a small strangeness, an opaqueness in Nyomah as she turns from the window in her housedress.

Esposito, Welch, and Lemm trace the Latin *communitas* in its derivation from *munus, which means "gift," or even "obligation," toward another.* Obligation is a threat to individuality, to subjectivity without rupture, thus a threat to freedom.

But what of the word *freedom*? Thinking through to the other side of it, what are the shadows and contraries there? Going back to the Middle Ages, a long tunnel of persistent thinking posits freedom as being rid of the thing blocking or binding oneself. Freedom meaning *freedom from.* But in the etymologies of the word—the Indo-European root for the Greek and Latin, the Sanskrit root for the English and German—all *recall something that has to do with a common growth.* Not a shedding or unfettering, but *a growth that brings together*, a blossoming from a shared rhizome. Freedom's origin is communitarian and grounded in relationship, *exactly the opposite of the autonomy and self-sufficiency of the individual.* The essence of freedom is not negative at all. *It has*

nothing to do with the absence of an impediment, with the removal of
a constraint, or with that which is exempt from oppression. Instead,
freedom yokes together.

In our desert era, we are fluent in the hollow language of rights
which is not the language of obligation, of gift. We move away
from the strange law toward the unimaginative law, the right of
an individual, rights to defend and keep secure. Protection of tribe
and identity and sameness, with duty to the other requiring only a
begrudging of rights, a bare minimum. We think this will save us,
but there's no nourishment in it. I'm more drawn to community as
thought through by Esposito, Welch, Lemm: *I intend community*
not as a locus of identity, belonging, or appropriation, but, on the con-
trary, as a locus of plurality, difference, and alterity. So, a *community*
that opens itself to the singularity of every existence. This is the experi-
ence of freedom.

Rights render the other as tolerable if kept at a reasonable,
safe distance; obligation envisions the other as the beautiful to be
drawn near in community.

Nyomah turned from the window a face I knew but could
never fully know. I'm not sure, but maybe my small self, on her
bike ride back across the cattle guard in a world so small that it cre-
ated and defined hereness, somehow registered the secret strange
life in Nyomah as a puncture in an insular world. I did indeed
learn to be member of a community in the place I grew up, but
not for the reasons I once believed. For there is an infinitely small
difference which is infinitely more than everything. I was a member with Nyomah not because of surface familiarity, but because
I was shown a glimpse in her unknowability, inside her house not
mine, of the fact that there would be faces beyond hers, bodies in
various dresses, with open eyes and troubled brows and longing
for food, all of them within her, though not her, and no less my
neighbor. And I was already bound to them, my freedom bound
up in their freedom, my beauty bound up in theirs. Native to for-

eigner, neighbor to stranger, all within our exchange of butter and ice cream delight. If I was willing, love overspilling the old citizenships would turn my face again and again toward the unknown, as if toward the rose of Sharon out Nyomah's window, the horizon pinked with evening coming on.

THE MAN'S EYES FLUTTER WET. He pulls back his hand from the hide. He is standing again in the shade of the cedar between the beasts at rest, as if he'd never moved into the stall or dreamed the bull-ox's dream. He blinks and blinks and smells their docile bodies breathing. Unwedges his body from between theirs and walks away. He almost starts to cry from a swell inside, as if fresh water were filling a channel that until now has kept its dryness secret. He watches the latchet of his sandals with a kind of astonishment as he climbs the hill, one step, two. Has he been changed by laying his hand to the coarse-soft hide? Maybe it's as she has been waiting for—he's been changed into himself.

They come to him as a gathering throng, people on blankets on the hillside. Their raw faces toward him, their backs bent, heads leaden and febrile. They are so tired in their gravity and disappointment and loneliness, the strictures and the nagging shadows of age and death. Then he sees that she is there, too, in the crowd, on the hillside among the broken sprigs and the hard dirt and the rock. The teamster's daughter, her hair braided back now. She sits on a dark blanket, pushing up on her knees to see, blue shift like lapis lazuli against black sand. She sees he is altered.

He finds the word *gentle*, he finds the word *lowly*. In his mind is the bull-ox speaking out to the deep *you* of the cow, the near one far drawn close. The man keeps hold of the idea of unlikelihood: the freedom in the downturn, the burden he will carry like taking wing, and carry deep into the heart of humanness. He is only beginning, just setting out on foot, but it is enough to clarify his voice projected out over the hillside, clear and with layers in it, and strong. "Come to me, all you who are weary and burdened, and I will give you rest," speaking a language they can both hear and see inside of. Only with the utmost attention, only with imagination, can they hear him say, *I love you, unknown in the known, strange one my beautiful one*, words that can point their raw faces toward the secret otherwise. Didn't he glimpse in the dream, really, the great ease of God? The burden of love without weight. He says, having learned from the beast, "Take my yoke upon you, learn from me, for I am gentle and lowly, you will find rest. For my yoke is easy and my burden is so light."

LEANING TO HEAR, THE TEAMSTER's daughter almost falls forward, her limbs heavy unto the earth but floating toward the shock of himself. The air is cool on her bare shoulder, like a touch from something invisible. She is light as a peahen asleep in a tree, in the branches of the acacia with its dark pith nourished by some hidden source in the scorched and desolate places of this world.

MAYBE IT WAS LIKE THIS. Who is to say it wasn't? Who is to say, in this great myth, that Jesus did not put his hand to the hot hide in the manner of the teamster's daughter, feel the miracle of stomachs, climb into the oxen's dreaming, and whisper *how are you possible* despite all that business of authoring life from the start? Stroke the nosebone to find his way by feel into the mysterious dynamic of ease and burden, freedom and boundness.

Maybe this was the dream infusing the phrases I heard as a slip of a girl in the pew when, in my jumper, I listened to the red-letter words of Jesus roll off late twentieth-century tongues. There was the song in our shape-note hymnal, "Come Unto Me," and the flannel-board Jesus, arms out, Velcroed to the hillside saying *come*, and here came the children and the old men, lips pooched out with dip, the women hanging up a phone, lips parted from speech, the people who had neither mat nor pillow nor book nor friend nor hearth nor legs nor sight. Couldn't we feel the flannel board growing wider and taller, bigger than the sanctuary, to fit all the Velcro throngs so tired, the hanging weight of their flesh like laundry poorly wrung? Couldn't we sense these were words with an inner world so vivid that—if we paid close enough attention—we could reach out and touch that world as one would touch the side of a laboring beast?

I KNOW THAT EVEN OUR BEST THINKING CAN'T SAVE US NOW. Teju Cole writes in *Human Archipelago*, on a page opposite Fazal Sheikh's photo of a refugee route through the Halutsa Sands: *We used to be like you. You could become like us. Our homes behind us, the uncertainties before us, and a current moment that is swollen like a sail. The truck moves like a laden boat. The planet is parched. The desert shifts in the wind, saying only its own name: desert, desert, desert.*

As I write this, nearly two million Palestinians in Gaza have been displaced by the Israel-Hamas war, over six million Ukrainians have fled Russian violence, almost seven million Venezuelans have fled their collapsing homeland, and one and a half million Syrians have been displaced by civil war to Lebanon alone. The United Nations predicts that 135 million will be displaced by desertification by 2045. There will be only more homelessness and shadelessness, and only an intensified tribalism to answer it, expelling the other and resisting the risk of hospitality. There will be only more desert; this we know is true.

As I write this, the kids attend their last day of fifth grade before summer, another storm has cleared and pillowed the far mountains with mist. I am a not-mother mother yearning for peace for these kids, for all kids. For their sake, I try to think through to the other side of peace. It is not the absence of burden. It is shalom in the midst of these wars, greening in the midst of dust and dust. Emmanuel Levinas said shalom means *not to close one's shutters, not to close one's door, but to put a* mezuzah, *a sign of welcome, on the door-*

post. Bring out meats and breads and fruits, while we have them, for those on the trucks. Then, tomorrow, it may be us on the trucks and if we have no food to bring out from our duffels, I will fill my hands with yours and we will pray this way.

And what is prayer but entering, unhelpably, the great girders of God's dreams? From the oxen I've learned to enter the dream with my full self, to let go of even the most useful thoughts and seek there an intimacy in the bosom of the one who is in time and otherwise than time, and thus to find my love there, too, and his children, and you, as you read this. In God's dream we may be more beautiful than we can fathom—the whole lot of us—and finally wise. We may simply be wonderful flashes of blue in God's dream, like the bright blue of the teamster's daughter's dress, or the open-mouth-to-drink blue, the flavored snow cone and all that blue-raspberry juice pooled in the bottom tip of the paper cone. Like the blue of the Mediterranean Sea at low tide when I crossed the earth to see it once, like the blue bar of my bicycle ribboned and hung with a wicker basket, blue of the tiles in the Moorish palace with bits of Arabic still visible and each letter blue-tipped with a horsehair brush. Blue pail in the goat shed I loved so far from the palace. Blue of the door to this small room where, emptied of hope and hopeful, I am reading an ancient text of the yoke and the feather, with all the windows open to the wind as I write.

ACKNOWLEDGMENTS

MANY OF THESE ESSAYS first appeared in literary journals and magazines, often in a slightly different form:

"Prologue" *Appalachian Review* (as "Yoke")

"Meet Me at the Dollar General Across from the Family Dollar" *Blackbird* (as "Meet You at the Dollar General Across from the Family Dollar")

"Blessing for the Lice Check" *Scoundrel Time*

"Bless the Smallest Hollow: On Longing & Online Dating" *Gulf Coast* (as "Blessed Be the Longing That Brought You Here")

"What I Want Your Voice to Do" *Blackbird*

"Sunday Morning Coming Down" *Willow Springs*

"A Story of Mary & Martha Taking in a Foster Girl" *New England Review*

"When I Dream Us into the Book of Ruth" *Arts & Letters*

"A Thousand Faces" *River Teeth*

"When the Season Is Fitting" *The Literary Review*

"Answer When You're Called" *AGNI*

"Screenporch As Prayer" *Portland Magazine*

BIBLIOGRAPHY

Meet Me at the Dollar General Across from the Family Dollar

Hillesum, Etty. *An Interrupted Life and Letters from Westerbork*, translated by Arnold J. Pomerans. Henry Holt and Company, 1983.

Bless the Smallest Hollow: On Longing & Online Dating

Bourgeault, Cynthia. *Centering Prayer and Inner Awakening*. Cowley Publications, 2004.

Finkel, Eli J. and Susan Sprecher. "The Scientific Flaws of Online Dating Sites." *Scientific American*, May 8, 2012.

Morrow, Susan Brind. *The Dawning Moon of the Mind: Unlocking the Pyramid Texts*. Farrar, Straus and Giroux, 2017.

One thing have I asked, that will I seek after, to gaze upon the beauty of the Lord and to inquire in his temple. Psalm 27:4-5, English Standard Version.

Percy, Walker. "Metaphor as Mistake." *Message in the Bottle: How Queer Man Is, How Queer Language Is, and What One Has to Do with the Other*. Picador, 2000.

Robinson, Marilynne. *Housekeeping*. Picador, 1980.

Zornberg, Avivah Gottlieb. "Introduction." *The Beginning of Desire: Reflections on Genesis*. Image Books, Doubleday, 1995.

What I Want Your Voice to Do

The Lazarus narrative is drawn from John 11.

Sunday Morning Coming Down

Goyen, William. *The House of Breath*. Triquarterly Books, 1949.

Hagar's narrative is drawn from Genesis 16.

Heschel, Abraham. *The Sabbath*. 1951. Farrar, Straus and Giroux, Reprint 2005.

When I Dream Us into the Book of Ruth

Ostriker, Alicia. "The Book of Ruth and the Love of the Land." *For the Love of God: The Bible as an Open Book*. Rutgers University Press, 2007.

Zornberg, Avivah Gottlieb. "Law and Narrative in the Book of Ruth." *The Murmuring Deep: Reflections on the Biblical Unconscious*. Schocken Books, 2009.

Mercy's Small Engine

The narrative of the anointing of Jesus is drawn from multiple Gospel accounts: Matthew 26:6-13, Mark 14.3-9, Luke 7:36-50, John 12:1-8

A Thousand Faces

Butler, Judith. *Precarious Life: The Powers of Mourning and Violence*. New York, Verso, 2006.

Cole, Teju and Fazal Sheikh. *Human Archipelago*. Göttingen, Germany, Steidl Books, 2019.

Lopez, Barry. *Desert Notes: Reflections in the Eye of a Raven.* Avon Books, 1981.

Moses's narrative is drawn from Exodus 33 and 34.

Robbins, Jill, editor. *Is It Righteous to Be? Interviews with Emmanuel Levinas.* Stanford University Press, 2001.

Answer When You're Called

Bourgeault, Cynthia. *The Meaning of Mary Magdalene: Discovering the Woman at the Heart of Christianity.* Shambhala, 2010.

Goyen, William. *The House of Breath.* Triquarterly Books, 1949.

Jacob's narratives are drawn from Genesis 28 and 32.

Mary Magdalene's narrative is drawn from John 20:11-17.

Merton, Thomas. *A Book of Hours*, edited by Kathleen Deignan. Sorin Books, 2007.

Miles, Emma Bell. *Our Southern Birds.* Scholar Select (public domain); original publisher: National Book Company.

Stewart, George. *Names on the Land: A Historical Account of Place-Naming in the United States.* NYRB Classics, 2008.

As If Already Always

Bourgeault, Cynthia. *Mystical Hope: Trusting in the Mercy of God.* Cloister Books, 2001.

Emmaus Road narrative is drawn from Luke 24:13-35.

Parables of the mustard seed and the yeast: Matthew 13:31-33

Once, Little Lion

Rilke's Book of Hours: Love Poems to God, translated by Anita Barrows and Joanna Macy. Riverhead Books, 1996.

Berry, Wendell. "The Gift of Gravity." *The Selected Poems of Wendell Berry*, Counterpoint, 1998.

Cixous, Hélène. "Bathsheba or the interior Bible." *Stigmata.* Routledge, 1998.

Cole, Teju and Fazal Sheikh. *Human Archipelago*. Göttingen, Germany, Steidl Books, 2019.

Esposito, Roberto, Rhiannon Noel Welch, Vanessa Lemm. "The Law of Community" and "Freedom and Immunity." *Terms of the Political*. Fordham University Press, 2012.

Robbins, Jill, editor. *Is It Righteous to Be? Interviews with Emmanuel Levinas*. Stanford University Press, 2001.

Sermon narrative drawn from Matthew 11:28-30.

Weil, Simone. *Gravity & Grace*, translated by Arthur Wills. 1952. University of Nebraska Press, Reprint 1997.